CREATING COMPELLING CHARACTERS

FROM THE INSIDE OUT

L. M. LILLY

WRITING AS A SECOND CAREER

INTRODUCTION

Like a lot of writers, my first attempt at a novel was autobiographical. I thought that would make creating characters easy. I could just use thinly-disguised real people. Later I realized that wasn't the best way to create compelling characters (or a compelling story, for that matter, at least not for me).

Next I turned to books on characters, which often featured actual or mental checklists. You can find tons of these on-line by searching terms like "characterization" and "character development." They are forms that read like job applications or resume outlines, if a bit more personal. They include questions like *What's your character's current job? Eye color? Age? Number of siblings?*

Introduction

That approach has never worked for me. I think because it doesn't feel real.

Think about the people you care about. For how many of them can you name their eye color? Or the number of siblings they have? More important, does either matter? (Unless you're simultaneously dating more than one of your friend's brothers, which might be the start of a good story.)

Sometimes I don't even get the hair color right for family members. My brother Tim went gray years ago, yet I still tell people he has red hair, which he did for most of his life.

What intrigues me about characters—those I write and those I love to read about—is what's happening inside.

What that character worries about, longs for, and strives for. How that character sees himself. What core beliefs influence how the character moves through the world.

The questions and prompts in this book are meant to help you create or decide what's happening inside your characters. Think of each chapter and subsection as a place on a map.

You don't need to go to every territory, but it's worth looking over the entire map so you're aware of different possible paths and destinations. Once you've done that, feel free to skip around and focus

Introduction

on the chapters that hold the most meaning for you, but I encourage you to read all of them.

∽

Spoilers And Simplicity

This book uses examples, including ones that count as spoilers, from these works of fiction:

Gone Girl by Gillian Flynn
The Dead Zone by Stephen King
Dark Corners by Ruth Rendell
Gone With The Wind by Margaret Mitchell
Pride and Prejudice by Jane Austen

There are serious concerns with the way *Gone With The Wind* portrays slavery, the Confederacy, and the KKK to list only a few issues. I've used it not because I agree with its slant but because the characters themselves — including their flaws, their values, and their fears — drive so much of the story. You need not read or watch it if you'd rather not. This book explains what you'll need to know.

I'll also talk about characters from other works, including Sara Paretsky's long running mystery series featuring my favorite fictional private eye, V.I. Warshawski, and John Sandford's *Prey* novels. These discussions are more general,

Introduction

though, and don't spoil any significant plot points or endings.

For the sake of simplicity, the book often refers to your "character," as if there were only one that matters. Unless I specifically mention the protagonist or antagonist, though, the questions and points apply to any character.

I'll also alternate between referring to characters as her or him, he or she, despite that a character can also be an it—a company, a town, a computer program. Also, some characters (and people) may not identify themselves as one gender or another. If that's true for one of your characters, feel free to substitute in your mind whatever gendered (or non-gendered) pronoun fits.

As you read, if you feel overwhelmed by the many topics and questions remember that you don't need to know everything about every character.

Some characters will walk on, say a few lines, and leave. While it's still a good idea for those characters to have a distinct personality rather than being a generic teacher, pilot, gardener, etc., this book is aimed at characters who are key to at least one scene or appear in many scenes.

And even for these characters, you won't necessarily need to flesh out every detail.

Introduction

What we're aiming for is enough that you—and your readers—feel you truly know and care about those characters and what happens to them.

You can handwrite your responses to the questions and prompts, type them, or simply file them away in your mind. I often buy a spiral notebook to scribble about characters or use scratch paper that I file away in a manila folder.

If you prefer something more formal, there's a workbook version of this book that includes spaces for your responses.

Even if you have no idea how to answer a question or fill in a blank, I urge you to keep reading. Your unconscious will be sorting through and trying out options as you move to the next section. When you return, you'll be surprised how many ideas you have.

Okay, ready to explore your characters? We'll start with their beliefs and values.

It'll be fun. I promise.

1
BELIEFS AND VALUES

You could spend all day imagining your character in different situations, and trying out scenarios is not a bad way to get to know your characters. For example, your protagonist is walking down the street and a well-dressed elderly woman holds out a sign asking for money. What does your protagonist do?

Some of these types of questions are included later in this book.

If you're like me, though, unless it's a scene for your novel, a hypothetical scenario can feel like an exercise. I can walk through a writing exercise much as I can sit down and play scales on my guitar. But all of us have limited time, and I'm not convinced it's worth practicing scales for hours if I've got a concert to perform tomorrow night.

The other issue with specific scenes is the many variables. Take the woman asking for money. Is she friendly in her approach? Aggressive? Does the protagonist perceive her as needing money? Has the protagonist just lost his job? Does he have hospital bills for an ill daughter to pay?

A single scene requires a lot of context. If I'm going to figure all of that out, I'd rather focus on scenes for a story.

For that reason, this book poses questions designed to reveal big-picture beliefs and values that will affect many aspects of your characters and their lives.

For many of these, I've drawn from the work of self-help/business guru Anthony Robbins, who has spent his career figuring out how to help people make the most of their lives. If you haven't read *Awaken the Giant Within*, I highly recommend it. Whether or not you find it useful on a personal level, it's a great examination of character.

In particular, it examines global values and beliefs.

By beliefs, I don't mean religious beliefs, though those might matter. Instead, we'll focus on your character's overarching views about life, people, and the world. Similarly, for values, you'll want to consider not only the "values" we hear talked about on the political front (such as "traditional values"), but personal values. As in, what is most important to your character for her happiness, well-being, and place in the world?

∼

YOUR CHARACTER'S Beliefs

An example of a global belief a character might hold is that people are generally honest (or generally dishonest).

Whether that belief, or any belief, is empowering or disempowering depends on the situation. A character who believes people are generally honest may be happy because he feels free to be open and honest and he trusts people enough to form close bonds. But the same belief could be disempowering if it leads him to put too much trust in a business partner who is embezzling.

Either way, people tend to see the world through the lens of their beliefs. If at her first job your character finds the supervisor overbearing and unfair, but at the next job your character thrives and works well with the boss, then the issue at the first job probably was that supervisor.

If your character gets a second job, though, and the supervisor is overbearing and unfair, and it's the same deal at the third job, and the fourth, and the fifth, the common denominator is probably the character's beliefs about work, people, teamwork, or herself. (You can read more about this concept in Jon Kabat-Zinn's **Wherever You Go, There You Are**.)

Similarly, if your character is well-liked at nearly every workplace, or is able to work with particularly difficult people, or enjoys every job she has, that person likely has global beliefs that influence or even cause that.

Does your character hold any of these beliefs?

- **The little guy always gets the short end of the stick**
- **Anyone with power is corrupt**
- **No one ever likes me**
- **Workplaces are full of gossip and backbiting**
- **Every person has some good in her**
- **Most people do what's right**

- Learning to get along with people is a worthwhile skill that makes life better
- It's more important to be kind than to be right
- Most people like me
- I can find something to like about almost any job/person/situation

These types of beliefs are global because they tend to influence not only job satisfaction but how the character views friendships, romantic relationships, volunteer work, hobbies, politics, and any other area of life you can think of.

What are some other beliefs your character holds about people?
Life?
Herself?

~

Your Character's Values

What we value drives all our decisions, from the friends we choose to the jobs we take to where we live or what types of families we have.

You don't need to know everything your character values, but it's one of the best ways to get to know or to create a character.

You can create conflict by starting with a character you're drawn to, figuring out that person's values, then choosing conflicting values for another character who opposes the first. This is important because without conflict, there's no story.

For example, if you want to write about a protagonist who highly values peace and getting along with others, you might give him an antagonist who believes that disputing every point is the best way to get to the truth or to foster the most honest relationship. This difference can create great conflict—and so spark a story—whether you're writing romance, horror, literary fiction, or any other genre.

On the other hand, if you have a plot but no characters yet, you can start with what values your significant characters would need to serve that plot.

In *Pride and Prejudice,* protagonist Elizabeth Bennet highly values happiness and love in marriage, as well as compatibility, having seen her parents' unhappiness. Those values place her in great conflict with the practical realities of her life. We learn on page one of the book that she is one of five Bennet sisters who will face homelessness and poverty when their father dies, as will their mother, as his estate passes to a distant cousin.

Nonetheless, Elizabeth, defying her mother's wishes, refuses to marry the cousin. The marriage would ensure she, her mother, and her sisters will be protected upon the father's death.

If Elizabeth didn't value happiness—or perhaps avoiding definite unhappiness—in marriage so highly, she'd accept the proposal to protect herself and her family. But there would be no conflict, so no story.

As another example, in **Gone With The Wind** Scarlett marries her sister's fiancé to get money to support the family's home. Why? Her highest values are saving her family's plantation and keeping her family from starving. She's sure that if her sister marries the man, his money will not go toward the family or their home but toward the sister alone.

Someone whose highest value was loyalty to her sister would make a different choice, as would someone who valued romantic love above all.

Love Scarlett's choices or hate them, does anyone doubt that she would marry her sister's beau in those circumstances? Not for a second. That's a character with strong, clear values.

What does your character value most in relationships?

For work (paid or otherwise)?

In her approach to life?

If you're not sure about these questions right now, don't stress about it. As we get further into your character's mind and heart, values and beliefs will emerge.

QUICK GUIDE: BELIEFS AND VALUES

- Global beliefs affect how characters see all aspects of life
- Figuring out your characters' global beliefs about work, love, family, and themselves is a good, quick way to get to know them
- Values drive your characters' decisions—remember Scarlett O'Hara choosing to marry her sister's beau to save her family's home
- Creating characters with conflicting values creates conflict

2
FIRST IMPRESSIONS

A good shorthand way to get to know your character's insides is to envision the character meeting someone for the first time.

THINGS YOUR MOM Was Right About

As a teenager, I often rolled my eyes at my mom's advice, especially about dating. But I learned over time that she was right about one thing. (Okay, lots of things, but one that's relevant here.)

People rarely behave better, or treat you better, than they do on a first date. That's when they're trying hardest to impress you. If someone can hardly say a sentence without snapping at you, leaves a poor tip, or drinks five martinis in an hour, it's only getting worse next time you go out.

So let's talk about first impressions.

~

THE COFFEE DATE

Think about how your character would behave on a half-hour coffee date with a stranger with whom the character hopes to later have a personal relationship.

Depending on your character's life situation, that could be with a potential romantic partner, a potential spouse's mother, or a new neighbor. It doesn't matter which, the point is what your character does and says, or doesn't do or say.

What three things would your character make a point to say?

These will be things the character believes will help make a good impression or believes the other person needs to know.

What three things would your character almost certainly mention without consciously meaning to do so?

Here, we're not looking for things the character would purposely bring up but those that always seem to creep into his conversations, even with strangers.

For instance, I attended law school at night while working full time. It took four years, and during that time I did almost nothing but work, study, and attend classes. I worked extremely hard, and I did well in school, and I was proud of that. I felt it reflected a big part of who I am and what I can get done.

For the first few years of being a lawyer, I almost always mentioned that in first meetings. (And, look, I'm telling you now.) I didn't make a point to do it, but it was such a big part of my life for so long that it always seemed relevant.

From the other side of the table, I remember a coffee date where a man I'd just met called his ex-wife a bitch and spent fifteen minutes explaining how awful she was. Even if true, those are things most people try not to lead with, and it told me that many future conversations would be filled with complaints about the ex, or that he wasn't over the ex, or that soon I'd be the one he was complaining about.

Which brings me to the things most of us know we shouldn't say during a first meeting, and that we intentionally hold back until we know a person better.

Creating Compelling Characters

What three things would your character take care *not* to do or say on a first meeting?

If your character is unaware of any comments or topics to avoid, why is that?

For instance, is that person so healthy and well-balanced that there's no need for caution? Is your character so sure of being liked that he never worries about making a good impression? Might this result from overconfidence?

∽

JOB INTERVIEWS

We'll talk more about careers, jobs, and money in Chapter Nine.

For now, though, ask yourself the same questions from the coffee date section about a job interview. If your character is a freelancer or runs a business, you can instead imagine a first meeting with a potential new client.

Whether and how the answers differ in a job situation tells you something about how your character divides aspects of life and how aware or not the character is of the differences between the professional and personal realm. It also draws out potential career issues your character may have.

Switch Sides

In the Coffee Date and Interview sections you looked at the situations from the perspective of your character seeking something: a good relationship, a romance, a job.

Now flip the situations. Send your character on that coffee date again.

What three things could the other person say that would cause your character to cut the meeting short, to never see the person again (if that's an option), or to brace for a long and difficult relationship?

If your character usually reserves judgment or gives people chance after chance after chance, these things will need to be more extreme.

If your character quickly bails even if everything is near perfect, it might be as simple as the other person ordering the wrong kind of coffee.

There are two ways you can flip the interview scenario. First, you can imagine what your character wants from a job or position.

For instance, if there is a lot of overtime involved, is that a plus or a minus for your character?

Creating Compelling Characters

What's the ideal company size for your character to work for?

Would your character rather work for a non-profit, a large corporation, a small business?

Think about these and other issues that might cause your character to conclude a job was not the right one.

Now imagine your character as the one doing the hiring.

What would immediately make your character strike someone from consideration for a job?

What would your character say about the work environment to draw someone in?

How truthful would your character be about the downsides of the position?

All the questions and answers in this section tell you a lot about what matters to your character and also how much self control and self awareness the character has. All of them will affect how your character behaves and feels throughout your story regardless whether you ever show that person in a work environment or on a date.

QUICK GUIDE: FIRST IMPRESSIONS

- People (and characters) rarely behave better than they do when trying to make a first impression
- Think about (a) what your character deliberately says about himself on a first meeting with someone new, (b) what your character almost always tells people without meaning to do so, and (c) what your character knows he shouldn't say or do
- What would your character do or say in a job interview?
- When hiring someone else for a job?

3

SELF-TALK AND DECISION-MAKING

One of the most significant aspects of a character is what that person says *about* herself.

We all know someone who could win the Nobel Peace Prize and feel like a failure because she didn't win it five years earlier. On the opposite side of the coin, one of my friend's spouses was so convinced of her own worth that after three years of being unemployed with no job offers she turned down a well-paying job because it wasn't quite in the six figures.

On the less extreme side, one character, when asked if he was generous, would think of an annual donation to a single favorite charity and say yes. Another might say no despite donating monthly to three charities and volunteering at the local soup kitchen because he'd focus on times when strangers on the street asked him for money and he said no.

These types of differences highlight how introspective characters are, how they evaluate their own actions, to whom they compare themselves, and how they process questions.

Character A may simply not give such questions a lot of thought. Am I generous? Sure, I donate to charity.

Character B may be more analytic, tallying in his mind all his opportunities to be generous and his responses.

Character A may be thinking of a more expansive definition of "generous" than is Character B.

Or A may have come from a family where no one donated to charity, making him very generous by comparison, while B may have come from one where donations and volunteer work were the norm.

Finally, A may be inclined to think well of himself and B may be very self-critical.

Self-Talk

Let's look at the overall picture of how your character evaluates her own actions.

Imagine your character makes a significant mistake.

What does the character immediately say to herself?

For example, "I always do this," or "I'm going to get fired," or "This will be really funny a year from now," or "It's not the end of the world, I'll figure something out."

What factors affect that?

Here, we're looking for the influence of family and friends, self-image, whether the character is analytic or not, etc.

Does the self-talk change after a day? If so, how?

If not, why not?

Does your character tell anyone about the mistake?

Who, why, and when?

Now imagine your character achieves an important goal.

What does the character immediately say to herself?

For example, "It's not that big a deal," or "Thank God I didn't screw that up," or "I'm awesome."

Creating Compelling Characters

What factors affect that?

Does the self-talk change after a day? If so, how?

If not, why not?

Does your character tell anyone about the achievement?

Who, why, and when?

These two sets of questions reveal (or help you create) how your characters feel about themselves. Knowing the answers will make it easier to write scenes on completely different topics, as our view of ourselves permeates everything we do and say.

~

WAFFLING, Waiting, & Other Decision-Making Strategies

The way a character makes decisions also is vital to who that character is, and it affects who works well as a protagonist or antagonist. These two main characters drive the story. If one or the other tends to drift along and go with the flow, that can make for a very dull tale.

In ***Pride and Prejudice,*** protagonist Elizabeth Bennet not only makes a quick decision about Darcy's first marriage proposal, she hesitates not at all in expressing her reasons and attacking him personally. She feels justified, and while she doesn't specifically set out to research his background, she has essentially been doing that for the first half of the book.

She also makes a lot of assumptions, without quite realizing she's done so. The second half of the book is in great part about her changing her way of gathering information and evaluating people and learning to make more thoughtful decisions.

If Elizabeth were more like her sister Jane, the initial proposal scene would have played very differently. Jane thinks the best of people, is cautious in expressing disapproval, and always looks for a middle ground. A more Jane-like Elizabeth might still have said no at first, but she probably would have expressed her reasons in such a way that Darcy might have addressed her concerns right away. Unlike Elizabeth, who in anger probably would have rejected any explanation in the heat of the moment, Jane would have been far more open to seeing Darcy's point of view.

In other words, there would have been far less conflict, and so far less story, if Elizabeth made decisions the way Jane did.

For this reason, much as I like Jane as a character, Lizzy is a far better choice for a protagonist. Her quick judgments and decisions drive the story, as does her willingness to express her opinions, including ones others might not agree with.

She's also, however, willing to revisit those decisions and admit when she's wrong, another decision-making trait that makes her a good protagonist.

Lady Catherine, in contrast, would be a poor choice, at least for a story like **Pride and Prejudice**. Once she's made up her mind, nothing and no one can change it. If she concluded someone was a bad person and rejected a marriage proposal, it's hard to imagine any circumstances that would turn that around.

On the other hand, Lady Catherine's decision-making process might work well for a protagonist of a mystery, thriller, or horror novel who needs to persevere through all sorts of obstacles to ferret out the truth, reach the finish line first, or vanquish the monster.

Use the questions below to start figuring out how your character decides things.

Imagine your character is considering changing careers, starting a career if the character doesn't have one, or beginning or ending a significant relationship.

Does your character enjoy exploring options or feel better once the decision is made?

Why?

How long does your character wait to tell anyone he is considering a change?

Some people immediately tell friends, family, or whoever is nearby, others need to be far along in the decision process before sharing. Others won't talk until they've committed to a new course of action.

Some people think by bouncing ideas off others. Other people fear being influenced too much by someone else's view or being too easily discouraged. Still others react to negative feedback by doubling down and thinking *I'll show you!*

What are some reasons your character does or doesn't tell others while trying to make a decision?

If the character does tell someone, who is that person?

Only a best friend/partner/spouse/parent? Everyone the character meets that day?

What does your character do to try to decide?

Research online? Talk to a lot of people? Write in a journal?

Creating Compelling Characters

How long will it take your character to decide?

Your character might be someone who needs to date a person a year before considering marriage or she might get engaged after a few weeks.

Similarly, the character might be quick to start new ventures or embark on a new career or might need a lot of research and thought to be comfortable.

Another thing to think about is that your character's answer might be different depending on what else is happening in life.

An obvious example is if the character's current job is unsatisfying and low paying, it might be a lot easier to seek a new job.

On the other hand, you've probably had times where you were unhappy but the prospect of change was equally daunting. And some people always hesitate to change no matter what life is like at the moment.

So ask yourself:

What could happen that would significantly shorten the time it will take your character to decide?

What would lengthen the process significantly?

What's your character's greatest fear about

making this change?

If your character were to contemplate a career change, how much time would the character spend on each of the activities below?

_ Researching/reading about the new career

_ Asking people questions on-line

_ Researching/reading about career change in general, happiness, or self-help

_ Interviewing people in person

_ Talking to friends or family members

_ Writing in a journal

Once your character decides something, how often does he revisit the decision?

Now let's consider a less significant decision.

If standing in a store, how long does it take your character to choose what shirt to buy given three choices in the same price range?

What factors affect that time?

For instance, is your character worried about spending too much or about dressing appropriately for a particular occasion?

For decisions major or minor, does your character worry about making a "wrong" choice?

None of these questions alone will unlock your character's decision-making process, but each one will give you a clue to that process and to who your character is.

QUICK GUIDE: SELF TALK AND DECISION MAKING

- What does your character say to himself about mistakes?
- About achievements or successes?
- How does your character gather information to make decisions?
- Who does your character talk to, if anyone?
- How long would it take your character to decide to change careers?
- To decide whether to get married?
- To choose a shirt to buy at the store?

4
THE SECRET LIFE OF [YOUR CHARACTER NAME HERE]

As we talked about last chapter, some people share freely with others what's on their minds and in their hearts, others are more reserved. This chapter will cover how much your character focuses on her inner life and what emotions are stirring there.

∼

Fantasy vs. Reality

This section is about where your character most likes to live. I don't mean in terms of geography, which we'll talk about in Chapter Eleven.

About how much time does your character

spend in his own mind and how is that time spent?

For example, most writers I know have active imaginations. They not only make up stories about fictional characters, they imagine what the stories of people they meet might be and often try out in their minds new endeavors before moving forward in real life. They also may spend a lot of time imagining and worrying about worst-case scenarios. (Not that I do that.)

Think about your character and whether most of that person's focus is on the here and now or on what might be, used to be, or could be.

A few questions to get you started:

Let's say your character has a first date tomorrow for dinner with someone he really likes.

How much time does your character spend imagining how the date will go?

Are your character's imaginings about how wonderful it will be or about things that might go wrong?

Does your character imagine conversations that will occur on the date?

At work on the day of an evening dinner date, how hard or easy is it for your character to focus on work and forget about the date?

Now answer the same questions about an upcoming job interview.

We've been talking about specific situations, and I'm sure you can think of more. Looking at the bigger picture, though, ask yourself:

Do people say your character is "in her own world?"

Or do people say your character "has her feet on the ground?"

Does your character mentally rehearse meetings, interviews, speeches, or first days at work (or school) beforehand?

If so, how often?

If not, does your character do something else to prepare? If so, what?

If not, why not?

∾

Anger And Sadness

Emotions that are viewed as negative or uncomfortable reveal a lot about a person. Let's start with anger.

How often does your character feel angry?

How quick is your character to express angry feelings?

How does your character do that?

What sorts of models did your character have for how to express anger?

What people saw their parents or other adults do when angry has a great effect. This doesn't mean your character will imitate that behavior, but it will make an impression.

For example, much of Nick Dunne's life in *Gone Girl* is dictated by his father, despite that the father barely appears in the novel. Nick's father had terrible anger issues, particularly toward women, and was verbally abusive. Nick struggles not to be like his dad but fears that deep down, he is. He makes many decisions about what to do so he doesn't appear to be like his dad, and most of those choices backfire.

Another character might do exactly what her parents did without thought or by deliberate choice. Still another might engage in a lot of effort, whether through therapy or self-help or seeking out different role models, to find healthier ways to express anger.

What does your character believe about anger?

For example, does your character find anger frightening? Empowering? Wrong? Helpful?

Now let's turn to sadness.

If your character feels sad about a specific loss, what will your character likely do?

For instance, your character might immediately call a friend. Or drink wine or take a walk or sleep for long periods or binge watch television.

What will your character think about?

Some people double down on sad moments, reimagining them. Others try to quickly move past the emotions by focusing on something else. Still others search for ways to "fix" things if it's possible, or to find meaning.

These differences in both thought and action are part of why loss drives some people apart. If one person grieves by taking time off from work (if it's possible) to feel sad and remember the loved one and the other grieves by jumping into new projects to distract from the difficult feelings or to feel in control, each can feel isolated and alone in grief.

If your character feels sad for a day or two for no particular reason, what would your character most likely do?

Some examples are physical activity, reading, talking to a friend, or trying to help someone else.

Whether or not you know exactly what your character would do in all the situations above, you should be starting to get a sense of how your character manages and views emotions that are often seen as negative.

～

REGRETS

One of my favorite television shows is ***Agents of Shield.*** In the fourth season, there's a story arc that turns on regrets. I won't spoil the story, but the theme is that our regrets are part of what makes us human and who we are.

What your character most regrets and how the character deals with that tells you a lot.

Some people most regret actions or failures to act that resulted in loss of personal opportunities. Others regret how they treated people or the quality of their relationships.

Some people spend a lot of time contemplating regrets. Others feel they did their best with what they knew and see no point in looking in the rear view mirror.

Some questions about regrets:

If your character could go back and change his main regret, would he?

Before saying an automatic yes, think about what else might change for the character if the cause of the regret disappeared.

For instance, let's say the character's greatest regret is not going away to college and getting a degree. If the character met her spouse because of remaining in the town where she grew up, or started working in the family business and eventually ran it, would it be worth potentially missing out on those things? Would the character believe that she would eventually find a way for those other parts of life to work out?

Does the character believe that what's meant to be is meant to be?

In other words, does the character feel that his choices don't really matter, the end result would be the same?

If so, think about how that affects your character's choices and how much control your character feels she has over life.

Fear

Probably more than any other emotion, fear drives people to do or not do things. It's why news headlines so rarely feature upbeat messages or say things like "999 times out 1,000 at this intersection, everyone obeyed the stop signs and no cars crashed."

Fear makes people tune in, click, or read because as humans we're wired to pay attention to threats. Our ancestors survived by being vigilant and alert to dangers around them.

Fear can be a friend or foe for your character.

Fear of job loss might drive a character to work hard, prepare well, and push herself to develop skills needed to get ahead. But it can also be so insistent it makes it hard to concentrate, causes overreactions, or inhibits the sleep needed for best performance, paradoxically making it less likely a person keeps a job or excels in an interview.

Figuring out your character's relationship with and reaction to fear can tell you a huge amount about your character. When Johnny Smith in **The Dead Zone** wakes up from a coma, he fears what anyone would in his position. He fears he won't walk again, that his life will never be happy again, that his aging mother's health is failing. He deals with all this in various ways, but mainly by working hard and persevering.

Later, when his psychic powers tell him politician Greg Stillson poses danger to humanity on an epic scale, he is caught between two fears. The fear of (a) committing a moral wrong and making the world worse by killing Stillson and (b) committing a different kind of moral wrong and allowing thousands or millions to die by not killing Stillson.

Johnny's fears are largely thrust upon him by the world, and they are in proportion to the actual threats.

At the other end of the scale is the protagonist in Ruth Rendell's **Dark Corners**. At first, his fear that he'll be held responsible for a friend's accidental death seems reasonable. He gave her diet supplements that contributed to or caused the death and he feels guilty, though he didn't intend for her to die and didn't know they could harm her. Had he spoken up right away, he might have been criticized in the press, but it's likely he wouldn't have been charged with a crime. Yet he's afraid to say anything.

The fear grows and eventually takes over the protagonist's life, driving him to more and more desperate actions when another character finds out and uses it to blackmail him. Eventually he commits murder, all to cover up actions that were never a crime in the first place, and all because he was so afraid.

What is your character's greatest fear?

This question isn't the same as what would be truly the worst thing that could happen to a character or even what that character believes would be the worst thing. It's what causes the greatest feelings of fear, and what, if the character thinks about it, raises the most anxiety.

It could be survival-based, such as fear of not having enough to eat, becoming homeless, or losing a job.

It could be about other people—fear that one's child will suffer, fear of losing one's spouse.

It could be a fear of saying the wrong thing, being embarrassed in public, or of being found out as an imposter.

What does your character do when feeling most fearful?

This question gets at your character's strategies for dealing with fear. Are these things the same as or different from what your character does if feeling sad?

If your character's greatest fear became reality, how would your character handle it?

What does your character say to herself about fear?

Even if your character's fears won't drive the plot, take some time to consider and answer these questions. Sometimes the strongest character motivations arise from fears that are below the surface of the character's mind.

Joy and Happiness

Story arises from conflict. That makes it easy to focus only on those emotions that create or result from conflict, such as sadness, anger, and fear. But happiness and joy matter, too.

First, the obstacles and trials your character faces can be all the more moving if the character is on the brink of happiness. But more significantly, knowing what brings your character joy, how happy your character feels and when, and what your character believes about happiness is intrinsic to who that character is.

What day-to-day events bring your character joy?

We're looking for moments here, often quiet ones, such as a thoughtful email from a friend or family member, taking a walk, or hearing a favorite song.

Does your character actively seek out and/or notice those things?

If not, why not?

Is your character happy now (at the beginning of your story)?

If so, why?

If not, what does your character believe he needs to be happy?

Would those things truly make your character happy?

Why or why not?

Are those things within your character's control?

If yes, what is your character doing (if anything) to become happy or happier?

QUICK GUIDE: YOUR CHARACTER'S SECRET LIFE

- How much time does your character spend imagining future events or dwelling on past ones?
- How does that affect the character's happiness?
- What are your character's beliefs about and strategies for dealing with anger, sadness, fear, and joy?
- Is fear more of a friend or a foe to your character?
- Does your character feel in control of life or at the mercy of outside events?

5

CONSISTENCY AND CONTRADICTION

One big caveat to everything in this book is that people are full of contradictions, or at least what look like contradictions. This means that if your character always acts one way or fits perfectly in a category, that won't feel authentic to the reader.

But, just to make your life as an author challenging, if your character acts contrary to the person you've established her to be, that too will jar the reader. In real life, if someone acts in a way that's out of character, we believe it because we see it happening. In fiction, we tend to think the author messed up.

So what to do?

Consider **why** your character's thoughts, feelings, or actions are atypical in certain circumstances, then include enough cues to the reader that explain or at least allow the reader to infer the reasons for the inconsistency.

∼

Fast Talking, Slow Walking (The Need For Balance)

One reason for what looks like inconsistency is the need for balance. Someone who travels the country giving business presentations and wining and dining new clients might come home on Sunday, turn off the phone, and spend the day in silence, speaking to no one.

A judge I know said when it comes to personal decisions—where to go for lunch, what movie to see, which brand of coffee to buy at the store—she defers to her friends or husband or whomever she's with. She decides things all day long. It's her job. When she steps out of the courtroom, she wants other people to decide.

One of my friends talks faster than anyone I know and often does three things at once (and is actually good at doing that, unlike most people). But he walks so slowly I sometimes think he's stopping to decide which way to turn next. That's his way of unwinding, as the rest of the time his life speeds along. I do yoga, he walks.

Think about how your character finds balance:

If your character were home all day with three toddlers, what books or interests or relationships would fill the need for interaction with adults?

If she works fifty or sixty hours a week at a high-pressure job and never takes a vacation, how is the need for recreation and fun filled?

What areas of life absorb most of your character's time and energy?

Is there something your character does to balance that?

If so, what?

If not, how does that affect your character?

If your character's life is radically out of balance for a long time, it will affect your character and your story. (It might even be your story.) Because one way or another, it will. If that weren't so, there wouldn't be so many therapists, self-help books, and work/life balance courses.

WHAT TIME IS IT?

Despite what I just said about therapy, there

Creating Compelling Characters

will be times in your character's life when balance isn't possible or when the character has chosen to be what's traditionally thought of as "out of balance."

In fact, there are some good articles out there about how work/life balance at any given moment is pretty much of a myth, and it's more about focusing on one area at one point and another area later. In other words, life is a long game, if your characters (and you) are lucky, and it's better to look at the big picture.

As one example, your character may have next to no relaxation time if she's starting a business while working full-time at a current job. Another character may do nothing business-related if he excelled at a high-powered career for a decade and now is taking a few years off to stay home with small children or to travel the world.

Each of these choices could result in a short-term lack of balance but long-term happiness. Or not, depending how it works out. Either way, the character's focus at the moment contrasted with that person's more typical day-to-day life is a wonderful place for conflict and so for story.

For example, a character normally cheerful and easygoing may become intense and easily angered if he is juggling a full-time job, caring for an aging parent, and parenting a teenager. How the character manages that or what results from the imbalance may be a story in itself or may be a good side plot.

Or imagine a young woman artist who meets a guy who is backpacking through Europe post-graduate school.

He might tell her about the corporate job he has lined up for the fall, describe the MBA program he just finished, and talk about the high stress he'll be under. But the guy she's meeting is relaxed and fun. He's hiking and bungee jumping and drinking wine. They're so happy they move in together.

Then he starts work. Suddenly the woman's living with an executive who spends all his time at the office. When he comes home, he's worried about work and exhausted. He doesn't have time for adventures or visiting museums or so much as a glass of wine after dinner.

She misses that guy she met. When she looks for him, he's nowhere to be seen.

Think about the main events of your story and your protagonist:

When the story starts, is your protagonist in the middle of "ordinary life"?

If so, what's a typical week?

If not, what's different now from a month ago or a year ago?

Are these differences ones the character is happy about?

Are these differences ones the character chose?

As the last question suggests, it matters how the current situation compares to the past and to where the character hoped to be at this point.

Someone who anticipated and planned for a caretaking role will likely be less stressed than someone who needed to adapt on an emergency basis. Also, if your character is the grown child who cared for an aging father and is now doing the same for a mother despite promises of other siblings to take over, that will likely cause more stress.

Even smaller atypical situations can give the reader context for what appears to be a contradiction in your character.

If a normally easy-going, kind protagonist snaps at her employee or, worse, fires her for a small infraction, that will typically pull the reader out of your story. But if the protagonist's car broke down on the way to work, making her late, and her laptop froze while she was finishing a handout for a presentation she's giving in ten minutes, and the employee's error means the figures for that presentation are all wrong, readers will likely empathize with the protagonist and read on to see if her day improves or she regrets her decision.

At the very least, the reader will understand why the protagonist acts as she does and wont' see firing the employee as out of character or a mistake.

∼

Stress

As the last example touched on, extreme stress can cause a character to behave differently.

A great (and extreme) example of this is Johnny Smith in *The Dead Zone*. When we first see him as an adult, he's taking Sarah on a date to a county fair. They like each other and have a good time, and Sarah is contemplating spending the night with Johnny.

Instead, Sarah gets sick from a bad hot dog. Johnny takes a cab home. It crashes. Johnny's injuries put him in a coma for four years. Sarah still cares deeply for him, but by the time he wakes up she's married someone else. Johnny's facing multiple surgeries to be able to walk again.

By itself, that would be plenty of stress to jar

Creating Compelling Characters

Johnny and make him struggle to be the happy, easy-going guy he is.

But Stephen King's not finished. Johnny discovers he has psychic abilities that only complicate his life. He's drawn into a police investigation. He helps catch a killer, but it ends in more tragedy. The publicity ends Johnny's chances for being a classroom teacher, as he's deemed "too controversial."

Eventually he learns that a candidate for president poses serious danger to the world. Now John Smith, possibly the most decent, likable character ever written, a guy anyone would trust and want to hang out with, is contemplating assassinating someone.

What's amazing is that we believe it. We've seen what a good guy Johnny is. But Stephen King puts him under a tremendous amount of stress, more than almost anyone could bear, and gives him strong motivation.

You don't need to use stress that extreme, but your character must be facing challenges or there's no story. If you haven't come up with a conflict yet, now's the time to start brainstorming. Start with the extremes and, depending on your story, you can walk it back from there.

Some questions to get you started:

Given your protagonist's life as it is now, what would be the worst thing for that person to face?

How would your protagonist feel the instant that happens?

What would the protagonist do in response?

Who is most important to your protagonist?

Name one thing that could happen to that person that would seriously affect your protagonist's life.

How would your protagonist respond?

What's your protagonist's best quality?

What is one thing that could happen that would cause your protagonist to veer to the opposite extreme of that quality?

QUICK GUIDE: CONSISTENCY AND CONTRADICTION

- Real people are full of contradictions, but readers may assume an "out-of-character" thought, feeling, or action is a mistake by the author
- Include enough cues to explain apparent contradictions

- <u>Reasons for contradictions include:</u>

- The character's overall need for balance
- The time in the character's life (is he caring for small children? is she juggling a full-time job and a side

business? is a character's parent ill or dying?)
- **Stress**

6

YOUR GREATEST STRENGTH IS YOUR GREATEST WEAKNESS

When I started writing fiction, the books I read on craft assured me it was important that I know both the greatest strength and the greatest weakness of my characters, especially the main characters.

So I dutifully sorted through different traits I saw as positive and negative.

I'd create a character whose strength was being kind to people and struggle with what weakness to give her. Should she have a quick temper? Be a bad listener? Be late all the time?

Nothing felt right.

Part of my struggle arose from simply being a new writer, and part of it from not having enough life experience (or at least not paying enough attention to the experience I had).

But a big part of the problem was the way the mandate was phrased. Saying you should know "both" your character's greatest strength and greatest weakness implies those are different, unrelated things.

If you think about people you know, though, that's usually not true.

One of my mom's greatest strengths was that she spoke out. If she got a bad deal in the store, she pointed it out and and demanded a response. If she was angry about something you did or said, she told you. You didn't need to wonder what she thought or how she felt or walk on eggshells trying not to set her off. She was very clear.

That was also one of her weaknesses. There are times when it's better not to blurt out what you're thinking. My mom's plainspokenness often hurt my feelings and those of my brothers. We stopped telling her things because while we knew in theory she supported our efforts, what she was likely to say had a pretty good chance of making us feel bad.

In *The Dead Zone*, John Smith has a strong conscience and cares a great deal for others. These strengths allow him to be a good teacher, friend, and son.

When he foresees a major disaster for the first time—a fire at a restaurant where a large graduation party will be held—he's able to persuade a parent to host a separate party to which many of the kids go. But he's unable to stop the party because he won't do something illegal and drastic, such as running a car through the restaurant while it stands empty that afternoon, which would stop the party entirely. People die, and Johnny is haunted by that for the rest of the book. He particularly blames himself because he'd made previous predictions that had come true, so he knew he was right about the fire.

In that way, his strong conscience was a weakness because it kept him from engaging in a lesser wrong to save lives. That conscience drives the conflict that results in the book's climax. Moral, ethical, good-guy Johnny is faced with what he sees as two impossible choices. Kill Stillson to end the threat he poses to the world, which is wrong, or allow him to continue as is, thus causing millions or billions of deaths, also wrong. Ironically, a man with less conscience would be less conflicted.

In *Pride and Prejudice,* Elizabeth Bennet's confidence in her own intelligence and outspokenness are great strengths and are part of what draw Darcy to her. But they are also weaknesses. In the first half of the book, she fails to examine objectively her view of Darcy, telling herself she's certain her perceptions are valid and failing to recognize the role her prejudice against him plays. She also speaks plainly of his faults when she has only half the information she needs.

A weakness also may stem from lack of a trait or ability that would balance and temper the character's strengths.

In *Gone Girl*, Amy Dunne's great strengths are her high intelligence and her ability to understand people and their motivations. Those qualities could make her excellent in any number of professions or businesses and also could make her an engaging and caring friend and companion. But she lacks the conscience or empathy needed to turn those strengths toward something positive.

Now when I create characters, I look for similar relationships between strength and weakness. The protagonist in my *Awakening* series always sees the best in people and is extremely loyal to those she loves. These are great strengths. Her ability to form close relationships and her good heart make people want to aid her in her quest even when her situation (a virgin pregnancy) strikes them as unbelievable.

But they are also weaknesses because they make Tara too quick to trust and too willing to give people a second chance. These traits sometimes come back to haunt her in serious ways.

What is one of your character's greatest strengths?

What's an action your character might take, or interaction with another character, where that strength comes into play (whether or not it'll happen in your novel)?

What's the downside of that strength?

What's an action your character might take, or interaction with another character, where that downside affects the character or the people around her (whether or not it'll happen in your novel)?

Strength, Weaknesses, And Story

The second drawback of the "know your character's strengths and weaknesses" is what it doesn't say, which is that **story matters.**

Gillian Flynn said that with **Gone Girl,** she wanted to write about marriage and when it goes wrong. She focused on "courtship as a con game: You want this other person to like you, so you're never going to show them your worst side until it's too late."

In Amy Dunne, she created a character who played that con game to the Nth degree. The strengths and weaknesses she chose for Amy had to fit that game. If Amy were not smart enough to pull off her schemes nor insightful enough to know exactly what to do to manipulate those around her, the story wouldn't work. If Amy had empathy for others, it wouldn't work.

In **On Writing,** Stephen King says his idea for *The Dead Zone* began with two questions—whether a political assassin could be right and whether a novel could feature the assassin as the protagonist.

King needed a strong reason for assassination, and John Smith's visions, which are proven correct repeatedly, serve that purpose.

Making the assassin the protagonist of an entire novel, though, requires more than simply someone with prophetic visions. We need to like the character, want to travel with him, empathize with him, and believe at least that he is convinced the course of action he chooses is the only one that has a real chance to save the world.

In other words, Johnny Smith's strengths and weaknesses all need to support this story and make it compelling and believable. So while Johnny's greatest strength could have been high intelligence (and he is smart), that's not the main strength. It's that he's a good person with a strong conscience.

This is not to say you can't start with a character's greatest strength and weakness and build the story around that. But even then, story matters. As your story emerges, you'll need to reevaluate the character to see if that person's strengths and weaknesses fit the story. If not, you may change the story rather than the character, but either way you need to be sure the character traits work with the plot.

What is the premise of your novel or story—that is, what's the main conflict?

Don't worry about writing it like a pitch or a sales blurb, just write it in whatever way works for you.

Do your protagonist's strengths and weaknesses heighten the conflict?

If so, how?

If not, what are three things you could change so that the strengths and weaknesses increase the conflict?

Ask yourself the same questions about your antagonist.

QUICK GUIDE: STRENGTHS AND WEAKNESSES

- A character's greatest strength is often the same as the greatest weakness
- Figure out the downside of your character's strength, or the upside of his weakness
- A weakness also can be the lack of a quality or trait needed to temper a strength (such as Amy Dunne's lack of empathy and conscience to balance her intelligence and ability to read people)
- You can choose the strengths and weaknesses of different characters to fit a plot, or you can construct a plot that serves the characters

7

WHAT CHARACTERS WANT

There's an old saying among writers that in each scene, your main character must want something, even if it's only a glass of water. That's because tension and conflict are what draw readers into a story.

∼

SOMETHING More Or Something Else
    I learned about character's wants watching the daily soap opera *All My Children*. (It was my brain candy on and off for many years.) The plot twists were outlandish, the characters often overblown and melodramatic, but I kept watching.
    Why?

Creating Compelling Characters

No matter how happy they were or what they achieved, the characters featured in the day's episode always wanted something more or something else. That drove each storyline because whenever a character is trying to get something he wants, and that something isn't immediately available, there's conflict.

The harder it is for the character to attain that desire, fill that need, or reach that goal, the more conflict there is and the more intriguing the character, and your story, become.

∼

WHEN FIRST We Meet

To see how the rule about characters wanting something plays out in a novel, look at the first time Stephen King introduces each character in **The Dead Zone.**

In the fourth paragraph of the book (in Part 1 of the Prologue), we see our protagonist, Johnny Smith. He's six years old at a skate pond "wishing he could go backward like Timmy Bennedix." In case we missed it, at the end of the paragraph King says Johnny "wanted nothing...except to be able to skate backward, like Timmy Bennedix."

A handful of pages later (after an older boy

runs into Johnny as he's skating backwards, knocking him unconscious and triggering his first precognitive flash), we meet the antagonist, Greg Stillson.

In the first paragraph of the Prologue, Part 2, Stillson is introduced as a "traveling salesman" driving a car with seventy thousand miles on it that's starting to wheeze. In paragraph two, we learn the back seat and trunk are full of Bibles and tracts he's selling. Right away, we know Stillson needs to make sales.

A few pages later we learn that Stillson's father belittled him as a runt who would never amount to anything. Now Stillson is a large, strong man who earns enough to take care of his mother, but his father is already dead and can't see it, fueling Stillson's rage. He kills a dog that bites him when he tries to leave his calling card at a farmhouse. He loses control, and recollects a time he lost his temper and beat up a woman.

We also learn that Stillson believes he is bound for greatness and knows his outbursts will derail him if he can't learn to control himself. He wants—needs—to get a grip on his temper and himself.

All of that comes out the first time we see Stillson.

Next, in Chapter 1, we meet Sarah, Johnny's

Creating Compelling Characters

love interest, for the first time. We quickly learn she is trying to figure out how deeply she feels for Johnny. She's struggling a bit because of how her last relationship ended, but she likes Johnny and finds him attractive.

He spooks her by leaving the lights out in his apartment when she enters and wearing a frightening Jekyll and Hyde mask that glows in the dark and appears to float. He means it as a joke, but it truly frightens her.

He's appropriately apologetic and kind, and by the time they leave for their date to the county fair Sarah has decided she wants to spend the night with Johnny for the first time. She lets herself be happy and have a good time at the fair, but King includes enough foreshadowing that we feel less than certain the night will end well.

We next meet the cab driver who picks up Johnny from Sarah's place (she got sick from a bad hot dog at the fair, so he's heading home). Despite being a minor character, the cab driver also is full of wants. He worked hard his whole life to put his son through college and feels shocked when the son says the president of the United States is a pig. He wants to understand his son.

The next character we see is Herb Smith, Johnny's dad, when the phone rings at two a.m. We know Johnny's been in a car crash and is in surgery, but Herb doesn't.

Right away, Herb wants something—to know the reason for the call. He's put on hold. In the following paragraphs, he now desperately wants something else—for the call *not* to be about his only son.

One last example involves another minor, walk-on character. A lightning rod salesman enters a bar/restaurant after a long drive. King describes him as a "man with a big thirst, and he stopped at Cathy's to slake it...." He goes into his pitch because he notices the building is made of wood and has no lightning rods, and he wants to make a sale.

The lightning rod salesman scene is an especially good one to read as an example of a character's wants driving a scene and keeping the reader engaged. The scene appears in the first quarter of the book, but the reader doesn't know why it matters. In fact, we won't see the restaurant—Cathy's—and its owner again until we're into the last quarter of the novel.

What keeps us interested in the scene is solely this lightning rod salesman, a fairly nice guy who first wants a drink and then wants to make a sale, attempts to do it, and is blocked by other patrons who make fun of his pitch.

Creating Compelling Characters

Imagine the first scene that features your protagonist (or any scene if you don't know the first scene yet). What does the protagonist want?

Answer the same question for the antagonist.

∼

THE REST Of The Story

Whatever we see a character wanting at the outset may or may not drive the whole story. Adult Johnny Smith doesn't remember the incident on the ice or the wish to skate backward, and even if he did that childhood desire wouldn't sustain a novel. It draws the reader in on the first page, then what he wants changes.

He loves and wants to be with Sarah, but he can't because by the time he awakens from his coma she's married someone else. He wants to walk again and to teach, but he must endure surgeries and rehab to get there. Later, after solving a series of murders, all he wants is to live a normal life as a teacher.

His final want, after he meets antagonist Greg Stillson, is to protect the world from Stillson, which means stopping Stillson from becoming president.

In contrast, Stillson's basic wants stay the

same, though they become more defined. In the first scene, he wants to make a sale, but his overarching desire is to achieve greatness. The desire for greatness continues throughout *The Dead Zone*, as does his desire to control his temper so he can get there.

In *Gone Girl*, Nick Dunne wants to understand his wife. This remains his goal throughout the novel, but his motive for wanting to understand her changes. When he begins dating her, he wants to understand her because he's falling for her, wants to make her happy, and is fascinated by her. Later, he wants to understand why she seems to have changed.

After that, he wants to understand her because he wants to get out of the marriage with a minimum of trouble, though he recognizes that will be next to impossible. When she's missing, he seeks to understand her because he feels he failed her. When he suspects she's framing him, he desperately seeks to understand her so he can outwit her and prove his innocence. At last, he does understand her—enough so that he persuades her to give up her scam and return to him.

The ending suggests he will keep trying to understand Amy on a day-to-day basis either so he can live with her and protect their unborn child or get away from her.

What is your protagonist's most important want/goal?

What is the antagonist's most important want/goal?

~

PROTAGONIST VS. ANTAGONIST

You're probably noticed something about the above examples.

The protagonist and antagonist are blocking one another's desires and goals. That creates the overarching conflict that drives the story. If your protagonist and antagonist have mutually exclusive goals—if one wins, the other loses—that's a locked conflict, and it's the strongest type of conflict.

The protagonist and antagonist can work against each other regardless how much contact they have. In *The Dead Zone*, Johnny and Stillson don't meet until the three-quarter point in the novel. (*The Dead Zone* is also a perfect book to read to see the five point story structure I described in *Super Simple Story Structure*.) But we keep seeing both as they face other conflicts along the way and struggle to achieve their goals. At first, their desires don't seem to conflict. But once they meet and Johnny has his vision, the goals become mutually exclusive. Johnny wants to stop Stillson from achieving power and becoming president. Stillson strives for greatness and aims to become president.

In **Gone Girl**, Nick and Amy have mutually exclusive goals, but we don't know what their goals are until well into the book. Nick wants to divorce Amy—first to be with his new girlfriend and later to be himself again and be out of her orbit. In a more overarching sense, though, as we talked about above, his goal remains the same throughout. He wants to understand his wife, to figure her out.

Amy wants to make Nick pay for not loving her true self or, perhaps more accurately, for not behaving the way she believes someone who loves her must behave. We don't see that for the first part of the book because we're reading a fake diary planted by Amy. Also, the "real" Amy later realizes that what she really wants is to make Nick behave as if he loves her.

In the end, their wants actually converge in a twisted way. Nick wants to behave up to Amy's standards, which is what she wants as well.

Creating Compelling Characters

Everyone's Against You

While you need a strong antagonist with a goal that conflicts with your protagonist's, other characters also should have conflicting agendas. That matters because keeping tension strong and readers engaged requires more than one character who opposes your protagonist, at least if you are writing a longer work like a novella, screenplay, or novel.

So when you're thinking about what your characters want overall, look for ways their wants can oppose one another and, particularly, ways they can oppose the protagonist.

That doesn't mean the other characters are evil, though some might be, or don't support the protagonist in a general sense.

In *The Dead Zone*, Johnny's mother insists what happened to him is God's will and that God has a mission for him. She thinks he doesn't need to keep undergoing surgeries and doing physical therapy because God will heal him. She loves Johnny, but her beliefs and desires conflict with his need to finish his medical treatment and build his body and his desire for a normal, happy life.

In *Gone Girl*, the police pursuing Nick for the

murder of his wife aren't evil. They may not even be incompetent. Most of the time they'd be right—the husband killed his wife. Also, Nick does many things, including lying to them throughout, that make him look guilty, and Amy is a genius in how she frames him. So despite that the police are seeking to solve the crime and Nick is innocent, they are working against Nick for most of the novel.

As another example, Nick's girlfriend is smitten with Nick. She creates conflict soon after Amy's disappearance not out of a desire to hurt Nick but because she longs to see him and can't understand him shutting her out. Later, she turns on him, but even through his eyes she doesn't seem evil. She appears embarrassed and guilty about her former conduct, and she wants to help the police.

Nick also is a great example of the person who lies to the police—and to others—not out of a desire to thwart them or because he's a bad person but for other more personal reasons. Nick believes telling the police about his affair will make him look guilty. He also doesn't tell the police that some mornings, including the one when Amy disappeared, he hides out in a garage and reads old issues of the magazine for which he used to write.

Creating Compelling Characters

He holds this fact back, though it would help him, because he's embarrassed and feels it makes him look pathetic.

As you plot and write your novel, look at each character in your protagonist's orbit.

Which characters are working for your protagonist?

Against?

Doing both, but in different ways?

As an example of working for and against the protagonist, Sheriff Bannerman in *The Dead Zone* seeks out Johnny, despite not truly believing in his psychic ability, because he'll do anything to stop a serial killer terrorizing his town.

But when Johnny identifies Bannerman's deputy, a man Bannerman thinks of as a son, as the killer Bannerman refuses to believe it. He gives Johnny all sorts of reasons why it's not true and punches him when Johnny pushes the point. Eventually, Bannerman is willing to question the deputy because he really wants answers.

So Bannerman works for or with Johnny because they both want to solve the crime and against him because of his personal relationship with the deputy.

To start thinking about this, or to sort out what the motives for and against are, list each of your major characters, what that person wants, and whether it means the person works for or against the protagonist (or both).

Character:
Goal/Desire:
For/Against Protagonist:

As you look at your list, if too many people are aiding the protagonist you probably don't have enough conflict.

On the other hand, if everyone works against the protagonist, particularly if they all have nefarious motives, you may have too much of a black hat/white hat situation. Try changing a few characters so their goals are ones the reader can identify with and root for despite that they are in conflict with the protagonist's aims.

Finally, remember that a character can have one goal that supports the protagonist and another that works against the protagonist. In fact, in my view, those are the most interesting characters to write and read about.

QUICK GUIDE: WHAT CHARACTERS WANT

- In each scene, the main character of that scene should want something
- Your story arises from your protagonist wanting something that is hard to obtain
- The strongest conflict occurs when your protagonist and antagonist have mutually exclusive goals or desires—if one wins, the other loses
- Some (but not all) characters other than the antagonist should have desires and goals that work against your protagonist, even though they may overall support her

8

RELATIONSHIPS

Whether your character is an introvert, extrovert, or falls in between, relationships of all types matter.

One way to explore relationships is to create a list, noting whether the character is married or not, has siblings, has children, has a best friend, has parents who divorced or stayed together, has step-parents, etc.

More important, though, is the nature and quality of those relationships.

In fact, the who of the relationships is often more a function of plot than character.

Johnny Smith being an only child serves multiple functions in *The Dead Zone*. It limits the amount of people he feels close to when he awakens from his four-year coma, lessening the number of people to whom he can turn with his dilemmas and fears. It adds to his concerns about his mother's health, as both his parents are aging and there are no other siblings to help care for them. It isolates his father during Johnny's coma, as he is having more and more trouble connecting with his wife, who is in the grips of religious mania.

The nature and quality of the relationships, though, is grounded in character. We see Johnny's concern for his mom and his attempts to connect with her despite that her religious exhortations disturb and upset him. We see the solid relationship of respect and caring between him and his father and draw conclusions about both because of it.

In *Gone Girl*, Nick's relationship with his twin sister, Go (short for Margo), humanizes him. Otherwise, as we move into the story, Nick appears so questionable that the reader easily could assume he killed his wife. He's frustrated and disillusioned about Amy, he can't deal with women who cry or get angry, and he's having an affair with a college student.

Because of Go, however, we see Nick through the eyes of someone who cares about him and understands him. Go gives us the side of Nick that he can't show to the world. We also see Nick, who otherwise reads as selfish and self-absorbed, caring about someone else. He and Go have each other's back, and they have fun together.

Your characters' relationships also reveal themes as to how your characters deal with life.

~

Conflict And Confrontation

As in real life, the quickest way to learn about your character is to see how she handles conflict with others and confrontation. On the most basic level, some people thrive on conflict, others avoid it at all costs.

But there are as many variations as there are people. Your character might get more logical and Spock-like as an argument escalates, or may quickly become distressed and find it hard to say what's on his mind. Another character might be afraid to voice her feelings and will dance around an issue or create other conflict to avoid saying what she truly feels.

Ideally, you'll want to mix these types of characters in your story. Otherwise, not only will your fiction seem unrealistic, it'll be dull. If your characters all shout at the top of their lungs when angry, every disagreement will devolve into people yelling, and that will become the bulk of your book. And if you have two people who avoid conflict at all costs, there may simply not be enough happening to add up to a story.

Despite that, as with any general rule, you can break it for a reason. You might create a fascinating story about two people who avoid conflict at all cost and the damage that does to their lives and relationships.

How your character deals with conflict also will depend on the situation and type of relationship, as well as on the concept of balance we talked about in Chapter Five. A protagonist who seeks out confrontation at work may balance that by being easygoing with family members.

Here are some hypotheticals to get you thinking about your character and conflict:

A friend who repeatedly chooses the same type of romantic partner only to see the relationship end in disaster asks your character's advice on how to improve his love life.

How does your character feel about this request?

Is your character concerned about how to

phrase any answer so as not to hurt the friend's feelings?

Why or why not?

What does your character say to the friend?

Another friend tells a joke your character finds racist, sexist, or offensive in some way.

What does the character do or say?

What if a supervisor tells the same joke?

An employee?

Your character feels his spouse is failing to shoulder enough childcare responsibilities after the birth of a second child.

Does your character make a list of examples of the unfairness?

Does your character arrange in advance a time to discuss the topic?

Does your character say nothing for months and then blow up at a minor scheduling snafu?

How accurate is your character's perception of the situation?

FAMILY

Your character's family ties, or lack of them, will be a big part of who your character is, whether or not that person realizes it. But figuring out the why and who and how is more than listing family members.

Some things to think about:

- **Your character's definition of family** (such as, does it include only parents, children, and spouse/partner? cousins? long-time family friends?)
- **How your character's family compares to cultural conceptions of family**
- **How your character feels about that**
- **How much time your character wants to and does spend with family**
- **Whether your character feels close to family members and why or why not**

Next there are the questions about why family matters, if it does.

Does your character treat family members differently from other people with whom the character has a close relationship?

If so, how?

If not, why not?

Does your character expect different things from family members than from other people?

These things could include financial support,

favors, a listening ear, understanding. It might also be the opposite of all those things if your character has had bad experiences with family or feels herself to be an outsider.

~

Family Dynamics

Whatever your character's definition of family, how he interacts with family members will determine how much they appear in your book. It also will influence the person your character is, even if the character never sees family.

In *The Dead Zone*, Johnny Smith is close to his dad, and he lives with him temporarily while he's recovering from his coma. Nick is close to his sister in *Gone Girl*. In fact, she's the only person he feels he can truly be himself with, so he spends a lot of time with her.

Amy, on the other hand, has a challenging relationship with her parents. Their *Amazing Amy* series puts her in a spotlight and also underscores, at least to her mind, her flaws and failings. In addition, her parents mishandle their finances and Amy has to bail them out, putting her own financial well-being at risk right around the time Nick loses his job.

Creating Compelling Characters

Nick has a difficult relationship with his father and is distant from him emotionally, but he is a key figure in *Gone Girl*. Despite that Nick rarely sees him, Nick thinks about him often, struggling with the ways he is like his father, and sometimes thinking or saying words his father would have said, much as he dislikes himself for it.

Is there a family member your character is seriously afraid of becoming?

Is there a family member your character has chosen to stay away from?

Is there a family member who refuses to speak to your character?

What family member does your character most admire, if any?

What is the most important thing your character learned from family?

What does your character deliberately do differently from her family of origin?

As with the other prompts in this book, you don't need to answer all these questions. You might not need to answer any of them. But considering them will get and keep the wheels turning.

~

DEFINING Family

Politics, at least in the United States where I live, often turns on how people define family.

Entire planks of political platforms are built on "family values," but what that means varies widely. To one person, it's supporting pre-school programs so all kids get a good start in life. To another, it's outlawing abortions and birth control. To another, it's getting violence out of video games or movies. To yet another, it's about embracing or excluding same-sex marriage.

As with politics, so it is with characters. Asked by a new acquaintance if he has a family, three characters who are all single with two brothers, one niece, a deceased father, and a living mother could respond completely differently.

One might say No because he's not married and has no children.

Another might say Yes and refer to his mom.

Another might say Yes and talk about growing up with two wonderful parents, loving his brothers and niece, and having a warm circle of friends.

In a moment, I'll ask you to write (or think of) your character's definition of family.

You can jump to that now if you like or you can first answer these questions for your character (assuming that character is an adult):

For your character, does family include:

Long-time friends?
New friends?
Godparents (if your character's religion includes that concept)?
Grandparents?
Siblings?
Parents?
Grown children?
Aunts and uncles?
Nieces and nephews?
The "greats" (great-aunt, great-grandfathers)?
Neighbors?
In-laws?
In-laws of in-laws (your character's sister's husband's sister, for example)?
Step-parents?
Step-children?
Children, parents, or siblings of a significant other?
Can anyone who was once considered family now not be seen as family?
If yes, how or why?
Who decides?
OK, now write your character's definition of family.

Categories Of Family

If your character's definition of family is narrow, perhaps including only a spouse or significant other and children, there may be no need to talk about categories of family.

Most people, though, consider at least some of the other types of people listed in the last section family. If so, think about whether your character distinguishes between types of family. Maybe parents-in-law are considered less close than the character's own parents. Or maybe it's the other way around.

Ask yourself the same questions from the Family section about each category of family and see if the answers differ.

Family And Society

How closely your character's definition of family and her actual family match cultural expectations is also significant.

The most obvious example, at least in today's culture in the U.S., is a character in a same-sex partnership or marriage. Depending where the character lives and her social circle and work environment, that couple might or might not be recognized as family.

If your character can't marry her partner, feels uncomfortable posting photos of the two of them at work even if others display photos of their families, or is discouraged by other family members from showing affection toward the partner (or perhaps from telling anyone about the relationship), that will affect not only the character's relationship with her partner but with her parents and co-workers.

Single people often deal with work situations where they are expected to work late or travel more because they "have no one" regardless of whom their social circle includes. Similarly, they frequently are expected to explain their personal choices in ways that married people are not. (It's rare for someone to say to a married person, "What's the deal? Why did you get married?" Single people, especially in certain age ranges, get these types of questions all the time.)

Similarly, couples who choose not to have children or can't have them often spend a lot of time fielding questions, including from complete strangers, about their lack of children. Many come to dread reunions and family gatherings for that reason.

Characters who are married may struggle with other people's views about their choice of spouse. Those whose families fit neatly into common categories—such as mom plus dad plus kids—may find themselves feeling guilty if they aren't happy or they wish for something different. They also may still be judged for their choices and asked (either directly or indirectly) things like: Why did you have only one child? Why did you have so many children? Why is there such a big gap in age between your children?

Any or all of these scenarios—or none of them—might apply to your character. The point is not so much that you choose one, nor is it that everyone with a similar family situation feels the same way.

The point is to give some thought to how your character's family is perceived by others and how that affects your character.

ROMANCE

No matter what type of novel you're writing, romance will be a factor, if only in its absence. This follows real life, where often one of the first questions people ask about an adult or young adult is whether that person is married or otherwise in a committed relationship.

How central a romantic relationship or lack of one is to your story, though, depends in part on the type of novel. In a romance, it is the plot. If a romance (or more than one) is a side plot, such as in Janet Evanovich's Stephanie Plum series, you'll need to spend significant time on your character's romantic life.

Even in stories where it's not a main part of the plot, you'll want to have a sense of your character's romantic relationships, particularly in a series. Part of why I like reading about John Sandford's Lucas Davenport character is that he is the type of guy who eventually married a super-smart woman surgeon who is as good at her job as he is at his. And before that, his relationships with women usually arose from a professional relationship and included both sexual attraction and mutual respect.

The relationships aren't the main reasons I read the books, but they do keep me interested in the character and say a lot about his confidence, the importance of work in his life, and who he is as a person.

In *Gone Girl*, while the book is suspense/mystery/thriller, the spousal relationship is really what the book is about. It raises question such as: Do we ever know the person we marry? How much bait and switch is there in courtship?

In *The Dead Zone*, on the other hand, the love between Johnny and Sarah is a side story. It makes the main plot more poignant, it adds to Johnny's losses and stress, and it gives us an outside/inside view of what Johnny goes through from Sarah's perspective.

Some things to consider about your character:

How important is it to your character, if at all, to have a committed romantic relationship?

What most attracts your character to another person as a potential sexual or romantic partner?

Are those qualities ones that contribute to a satisfying or healthy emotional relationship as well?

If yes, how?

If no, why not?

Are there patterns your character repeats in romantic or sexual relationships?

If so, how do those patterns affect the quality of your character's life?

What traits would your character say are most important in a potential long-term romantic partner?

Why?

Are those the same qualities your character actually looks for?

If not, why not?

If your character is married, is the spouse also the best friend?

~

FRIENDSHIP

Your characters' friends say a lot about that person and give the reader different perspectives on him.

The Why of friendship is as important as the Who. For example, if your character is forty and has known most of her friends since grade school, it could be because:

- she feels deep loyalty to those she cares about
- she makes a lot of effort to maintain friendships
- she hasn't expanded her horizons much or fears change
- all of the above

When you're creating your character's friends,

think about them as a whole as well as individually. Your character may like or dislike being around people with backgrounds (education, social class, neighborhood) or demographic characteristics (age, race, ethnicity) similar to her own, may want friends who always cheerlead or agree, might seek out those who strongly disagree or will call the character out for flaws, or may mostly associate with others in the same profession or place in life or seek out those with different life experience.

When you look at friends one-by-one, you'll need to develop those characters that matter most. Doing so will help you understand your main character whether or not the closest friends ever appear in the book.

Despite that, in my view, it's not necessary to dig deeply into every friend your character might have. Some writers believe in a backstory even for characters with one line, and perhaps in a perfect world you'd know everything about everyone who touches your main characters' lives.

But given the limits most of us have on our time, if you prefer to focus on one or two close friends and understand just enough to make the others real in the moments they appear, I think that's fine.

Creating Compelling Characters

Some questions to get you started:

How many people does your character consider to be close friends, if any?

You don't need an exact number. We're looking more for an approximation—one, a handful, twenty?

What needs to happen for your character to feel a friend is "close?"

One character may consider anyone she talks with more than once a week close. Another may need to talk once a day. Still another may not consider how much contact there is but how at ease she feels talking with that person. Yet another may care most about shared experiences.

Do you see how this question pulls out aspects of your character that you might not otherwise get to?

Does your character spend holidays with friends?

If a friend needed a favor, what factors would influence whether your character would agree to do it?

Are there any friends that your character would help out with anything anytime?

If so, who and why?

If not, why not?

Weak Ties

When you create your characters, they become more well-rounded if you look beyond the relationships we've covered above to whether they have a larger social network. In fact, less serious relationships can have a huge effect on your character's life and how the reader sees him.

This is one part of character where numbers matter. In real life, the "weak ties" a person has usually have more to do with business and financial success than do close relationships, at least according to most business and networking books.

This makes sense. If you have a hundred people who know you well enough to have a good general impression of you, you're in a much better position to find a new job than is someone who has only twenty people in that category. This is true even if the two of you have the exact same number of close friends and family members.

A large number of acquaintances also means a wider pool to draw from if a character wants to make new friends, find a romantic partner, or connect with others who share his interests.

As you think about your character's social network, also consider what works for your plot.

Creating Compelling Characters

When I started my *Awakening* series, protagonist Tara had a limited social network. She spent a lot of time with her siblings and parents. Though a college student, because of the family situation she lived at home. Also, her best friend was her boyfriend's sister.

I chose this background partly because it created more conflict for Tara. When her parents don't believe her about the nature of her supernatural pregnancy, it's particularly devastating because she was so close to them. When the boyfriend and his sister also don't believe her "story" on how she got pregnant, she's left with no one on her side. That makes her far more likely to turn to a stranger for help despite misgivings about him.

In contrast, in a new mystery series I'm starting, my protagonist is a lawyer and former stage actress with a wide network of contacts. These connections mean she has many resources to draw from when she starts investigating the death of the man she was about to move in. Without that network, it would be unrealistic to think she could investigate a murder given that she has no police or detective training.

Ask yourself these questions about your character's social network:

About how many people does your character know well enough to contact at least once a year?

Ten, one hundred, one thousand?

If your character hosted a business networking event, how many people would be on the guest list?

If your character works, does volunteer work, or serves on committees outside the home, how do colleagues, subordinates, and supervisors describe the character?

Colleagues:

Subordinates:

Supervisors:

Would your character agree with the things these other people say? Why or why not?

QUICK GUIDE: RELATIONSHIPS

- Focus on the nature and quality of your character's relationships rather than listing family members, friends, etc.
- Think about how your character defines family and how society sees that family
- Compare the qualities your character looks for in a long-term romantic partner (if your character wants that type of relationship) to the types of people your character is attracted to
- Figure out what causes a character to consider someone a friend

- **Your character's network of "weak ties" (acquaintances) will have significant influence on her life**

9

MONEY AND WORK

Your character's relationship with money also matters.

I call it a relationship because people's finances hit on all the same emotional issues as family, romance, and friendship. If that weren't so, there would be a lot more financially stable people in the world.

Jobs and careers are closely related to money because unless you write only about those who inherit wealth, your characters will need to earn money somehow.

Money Money Money

Money has a lot of layers. It has a practical and literal meaning. Unless your character lives in a society that is all barter, she needs money to survive.

Money also places a value on things, work, and—in some people's minds—people.

The average Major League baseball player in the U.S. as I write this earns about $4.47 million a year, while the average salary for a high school teacher in the U.S. is $47,760. You can argue about whether or not this means our culture actually values ball playing more than teaching and what other factors go into those salary differences.

For the purpose of building your characters, though, this simple statistic hints at many important questions.

For instance:

If the amount your character earns per year is zero, does that affect her self-esteem?

What if it's in the top 1%?

What if it significantly increases or lowers one year?

What if it's higher or lower than the character's best friend, sibling, spouse, grown child, or parent?

What does the amount earned per year mean to your character?

Ask yourself the same questions about your character's net worth.

Money might be how your character measures success.

It also might be a measure of good or evil. To one person, being well-to-do financially might mean being a good person who is showered with the bounty of God or the Universe. To another, it might symbolize selfishness or greed and signal underhanded dealings.

Money can serve as a proxy for love, which is why some wills and trusts lawyers advise clients to leave an exactly equal amount to each child, regardless of circumstance. Going back to our ballplayer/teacher comparison, parents whose only real asset is a modest house may look at their baseball player child and think it's ridiculous to leave him half of it. It will be a drop in the bucket to him, while leaving the entire house to the high school teacher child might cover a grandchild's college bills, be much needed to supplement a retirement fund, or fund a move to a nicer neighborhood. But giving everything to one child, even when the other is in excellent shape financially, can create bitter, "Mom always loved you more" feelings.

The best way to figure out how your character

feels about money is to ask what he would do in a dispute over money. Let's say your character gave a sibling $5,000 two years ago to help pay for a child's car or tuition. Your character believes it was a loan, the sibling says it was a gift. Your character absolutely does not need the money. (You can switch the amount to $100 or $1,000 if that's more realistic.)

If the dispute is never resolved, how long will your character think about it or talk about it?

Would your character consider talking to a lawyer or suing to get the money back?

Would your character ask for the money from the college student/car buyer?

Would your character stop speaking to the sibling?

If your character says, "it's not the money, it's the principle of the thing," what is the principle?

These issues overlap into family, and that's part of the point. If money means love, success, who is right or wrong, who is honest, etc., that's magnified when it's someone with whom the character has a personal relationship.

For Richer Or Poorer

Creating Compelling Characters

This section is not specifically about marriage, though the slightly misleading title might make you think so.

It's about relativity, relationships, and history.

Years ago an estate planning attorney told me a story about a client he had to convince to cut spending to live within a tighter budget. Every week she spent a fortune on sheets because she bought sets that cost thousands of dollars and threw them out after sleeping on them for a few days. She "needed" fresh sheets every few days, and laundering them just wouldn't do. It took him a long time to persuade her that she could either buy less expensive sheets or learn to sleep on ones that had been washed.

That client was an heiress whose trust fund investments weren't doing as well as she'd expected. Her idea of cutting back shows an extreme example of relativity.

But scores of less dramatic reasons exist for a character's views on money. Grandparents raised in the Great Depression, excelling in a lucrative career, job loss, having a radically more or less successful sibling, marrying someone with more or less money, or associating with people who have more or less money are just a few.

Whether you've figured out all these background details or not, some big picture questions are:

What is "enough" money to your character?

Is there an amount that would make your character feel rich?

Feel poor?

Is your character afraid of losing whatever amount of money he has?

Afraid of never earning enough?

If you're unsure or you want to draw out more about your character's feelings about money, imagine how a significant change in financial circumstances would affect that character.

For example, in *Gone Girl*, right after Nick and Amy both lose their jobs, Amy's parents come to Amy, say they've mismanaged their money, and ask her to give them nearly all of her trust fund. She says yes before even talking with Nick about it.

Because she does this, she feels she can't protest when Nick insists they move to his hometown in Missouri, a place Amy hates. But it's cheaper to live there, neither of them has a job, and New York offers neither of them any prospects.

Nick, too, finds the change stressful. After holding his own in Manhattan, where it seems to

Creating Compelling Characters

Nick everyone but him grew up going to prep school and playing LaCrosse, Nick returns home after losing his job. He's there in part to care for his mother and to open a bar with his sister, but he needs the last of Amy's money to start the bar. He feels like a failure. He starts seeing a college student partly because she sees him as this amazing magazine writer from New York, not someone who lost his job and can't afford living there anymore.

These conflicts over money set the stage for and reflect the other more dangerous conflicts in their marriage.

If something similar happened to your character, how would he react?

Your Character's Financial IQ

What your character does about money tells you a lot about her or, if you look at it another way, reflects a lot about that character. A person's money management strategies are affected by their feelings about themselves, what they learned from their parents, and what their main fears are. A person's earnings and net worth at a particular time give you a snapshot of other parts of life, including career, marriage, and family.

How much you need to know depends on your plot. In *Gone Girl* money was on on-going conflict for Nick and Amy. In *The Dead Zone* it added tension for Johnny and his parents because they faced long-term catastrophic medical bills, but it didn't drive the plot. It's at the heart of *Pride and Prejudice* because Mrs. Bennet and her daughters will become homeless when Mr. Bennet dies, meaning the Bennet daughters must marry, and some must marry men of wealth, to have a tolerable existence.

Below are some questions to draw out your character's approach to money. You're not limited to one answer for any of them, and you can write in your own response if none of the options fit.

If your character hoped to buy a new (or newer) car next year, would she:

- Look into financing options
- Save a certain amount per week for a down payment
- Save a certain amount per week to reach the entire purchase price
- Take a side job to earn extra money
- Decide it's out of reach after thinking about it for a while
- Assume the next year's raise or bonus

would be enough to cover it and start looking now
- Ask family for money

If your character won $200,000 in the lottery, would she:

- Invest most or all of the money in stocks, real estate, or bonds
- Give some to family members right away
- Spend most of the money over the course of the year on vacations, clothes, and a new car
- Renovate or buy a home
- Spend the money over the next year or two but never be quite sure where it went
- Sit down a day after winning and make a detailed plan on what to do with it
- See a financial advisor before spending anything
- Ask a friend, spouse, or family member for advice on spending
- Buy into a "can't miss" scheme to

double or triple the money and end up losing it

If your character is married, how much input would the spouse have in how the lottery money is spent?

Your character's expenses are exceeding income by a hundred dollars a month. Which of these might your character do?

- Ask for a raise (if employed) or raise rates (if an entrepreneur or freelancer)
- Look for more business (if an entrepreneur or freelancer)
- Work more hours
- Assume he will catch up next year with a raise or bonus and borrow until then
- Get another credit card or two
- Ask family for help
- Look for a new job
- Take a side job
- Figure out expenses to cut
- Move to a cheaper living situation
- Buy lottery tickets or take a gambling trip

- Start a side business
- Go back to school or take classes to develop new skills
- Spend the same or more each month and pray for a windfall

Imagine your character earns about $200 a month more than her expenses. What does she typically do with that money?

About how much of what your character earns does he save per year? (If your character is married and the spouse earns the money for both, answer for the couple.)

Does your character:

- Have a checking account?
- Have a savings account?
- Owe money on credit cards? (If so, how much?)
- Have an emergency fund?
- Have a mortgage?
- Have a car payment?
- Feel fairly compensated for her work?
- Set financial goals each year?
- Set any financial goals?
- Achieve financial goals?
- Feel safe financially?

- Worry about money?
- If yes on worry, are the fears realistic?
- Spend easily?
- Count every penny?
- Tip well at restaurants?
- Shop for bargains?
- Buy secondhand clothes?

∼

Social Class and Money

This section could easily fit in the next chapter on demographic factors. I'm including it here because there often exists a strong interplay between money and social class.

Even in the U.S., where there is a strong belief in social class mobility and people's ability to go from rags to riches, most people stay in roughly the same social and economic class as did their parents.

Further, a large percentage of people do for a living what their parents did. Children of teachers are more apt to become teachers than their peers are, actors to become actors, lawyers to become lawyers.

Plenty of conflict can arise either way. A character who follows in a parent's footsteps may for-

Creating Compelling Characters

ever feel in the parent's shadow or, conversely, forever feel the need to prove he can succeed where the parent failed. Going into business with parents adds more complications.

Conflict also occurs when people move from one social class to another. These people are sometimes called straddlers. They have a foot in both worlds, but feel somewhat out of place and fearful of doing the wrong thing in either place.

Gone Girl and ***Pride and Prejudice*** both deal with social class mobility.

Nick Dunne's life includes conflicts because he's from a blue collar background. He becomes a writer in New York, where most people he meets are more well off and grew up differently than he did, and marries a woman who is not uberrich but who is comfortable financially whether she works or not. (At least until her parents raid her trust fund.)

When Nick returns to his hometown, though, he feels out of place there as well. He realizes he's been looking down on the people there, feeling like he's smarter than they are. One of his friends resents Nick's success and is quick to reinforce his feeling that he's a failure because he moved back.

In ***Price and Prejudice***, Jane and Elizabeth run into prejudice against them both because of their father's lack of an estate of his own and because their parents don't enforce the accepted social class manners and traditions on the younger daughters. Darcy's aunt is also appalled by Elizabeth's lack of connections and lack of nobility and frankly tells her Darcy's estate will be "polluted" by Elizabeth's presence.

How does your character feel about where she is economically and socially?

Does your character hope to one day belong to a different socioeconomic class?

Has your character recently been through a perceived change of socioeconomic class?

If so, how does the character feel about that?

How have friends and family reacted?

W*ORK* E*THIC* **and Orientation**

A lot of factors go into what type of work your character does.

You may be drawn to certain professions or jobs, making it fun to write about them. Or you may know something about a career and can cut back your research by assigning it to a character. Your plot may demand that your character possess knowledge or expertise.

Setting these factors aside, when creating a character the actual type of work is less important than his approach to it. Professor Wayne Baker and people analytics manager Kathryn Dekas use three categories to describe different types of work ethic.

Do any of these fit your character?

A job-oriented person works to get the paycheck and looks for life satisfaction in other places.

This character can still work very hard and be good at a job, but that's not what she is really engaged in. The job fills 9-5 (or whatever shift), but once the work shift is over, it's over.

Or, as my mom used to say, do you live to work or work to live? The job-oriented character works to live.

A career-oriented person is most concerned with advancement. Dekas and Baker say this type of person might not work as effectively in teams as a result of being more focused on personal success than that of the group.

On the other hand, your character might need the team to succeed to achieve personal success, or might want to do well personally but also be invested in the success of others. Either way, though, the career-oriented character has or wants work that is part of a larger picture, not a job that is about clocking out (literally or figuratively) at the end of a shift.

A calling-oriented person wants to have a positive impact on the world or others and/or finds—or hopes to find—personal fulfillment in work. These characters are often ones that would work in this same field even if they didn't get paid.

Many calling-oriented people work long hours because they are dedicated to the work and usually are satisfied with it.

Johnny Smith in *The Dead Zone* is a great example of a calling-oriented character. He loves teaching. He wants to earn his living doing it, and he wants it as his career, but he is happiest when he feels he's truly helped a student or students.

Nick Dunne is career-oriented. A lot of his self-image is invested in being a writer for a New York magazine, and when he loses that he feels lost. So lost that he hides in a garage reading back issues when he feels particularly low.

Your character doesn't need to fit neatly into one of these categories. Amy Dunne doesn't, though she is probably the closest to career-oriented. She likes writing quizzes and she likes having a job and feels irritated when Nick downplays it. She doesn't need to work, so she's not someone punching a clock simply to earn wages. She doesn't see her work as a calling. But work matters to her. It's part of her identity.

Any of these approaches can have pluses and minuses and can add to or take away from your character's happiness.

One character in a 9-5 job with few prospects for advancement might be thrilled if it pays the bills, allows time to pursue hobbies, and/or allows him to start a weekend business or to travel. Another might find the work dull or feel too exhausted on returning home at night and feel the pay doesn't fairly compensate for the hard work.

If your character is calling-oriented or career-oriented, she might find the work challenging or exciting but end up working too many hours and becoming burned out or miss too much time with family and friends.

Also, a character's focus can change depending on what else is happening in her life. A character who runs her own business for decades might consider it a break to go back to a 9-5 job and truly enjoy it.

Even if you don't know yet what work your character will do and whether it will be paid or unpaid, ask yourself a few questions:

What sort of work would your character do even if he would never get paid for it?

Does your character prefer to have the type of job she won't need to think about when not at work?

Does your character prefer working the same hours each day or week?

Would your character enjoy working from home?

Would your character rather work for someone else, be self-employed, or start and manage a business?

How does your character feel about changing careers or jobs?

How would your character feel if she lost a long-time job?

QUICK GUIDE: MONEY AND WORK

- Your character's relationship with money reflects many of her beliefs and values, including about herself
- Think about what money represents to your character: Success? Love? Happiness? Morality?
- What is "enough" money for your character?
- How does your character differ from his family of origin, if at all, as to money, social class, or work?
- What type of work ethic does your character have?

10

INF WHAT? (USING PERSONALITY TESTS)

Theories of personality, and related tests or questionnaires, regardless whether you think them valid in real life, are rich mines for creating characters.

These theories can also help you create conflict without relying on a too-perfect hero or mustache-twirling villain. By creating two characters who occupy opposite places on personality trait spectrums, you create conflict.

I've found especially helpful the personality type theory of C.G. Jung as used in the work of Isabel Briggs Myers and Katharine C. Briggs. (Any errors in the discussion below, which reflects my layperson's understanding, are solely my own.

Creating Compelling Characters

Also, while Jung spelled *extraverted* with an *a* rather than an *o* in the middle, I've opted to use the more common layperson's spelling throughout.)

The four aspects of personality Myers and Briggs talk about are:

- Extroverted/Introverted (E or I)
- Intuiton/Sensing (N or S)
- Thinking/Feeling (I or F)
- Perceiving/Judging (P or J)

The resulting combination of all four factors is identified by initials. For example, the last time I took a personality inventory based on this work, I was an INFJ (Introverted, Intuition, Feeling, Judging), though on three of the factors I scored very near the center. (Critics argue that many people do, particularly on the E/I scale.)

The inventory for Extroverted/Introverted includes questions such as whether you feel energized or drained after going to a party with a lot of people. The more energized, the more likely you are to be an extrovert. The more drained, the more likely you're an introvert.

Also, if you unwind and recharge by being with other people, you're more likely to be an extrovert. If you recharge by spending time alone, you're more likely an introvert.

I found this part of the inventory fairly accurate for me as someone in the middle but on the Introvert side. I like to talk to people and enjoy public speaking, so long as I am well-prepared and know my topic, but after a day interacting with people I want to go home and read a book, write, or take a walk alone.

Intuition versus Sensing is a little less obvious. Basically, the theory is that people on the Intuition (or N) side look mainly at the big picture and interpret and add meaning to the information they take in. Sensors focus more on "just the facts" and may be more literal.

So two people who belong to the same religious faith and share many beliefs could argue frequently if on the opposite ends of this spectrum. To your S character, the most important parts of religion might be knowing and observing specific rules and formalities. An N character, in contrast, would care more about what overall doctrine means and how it affects the people who follow it and the world. Character S might feel the only way to "honor the Sabbath" is to do or not do certain specific things, while Character N might see multiple ways to do that, including unconventional ones.

Neither would be wrong or right, but there might be a great deal of conflict between them.

Thinking/Feeling is more or less how it sounds. Those on the T side are more likely to approach issues and decisions in an analytic way. They will likely speak that way as well, saying, "I think..." or "Statistics show..." or "It makes sense that..."

Feelers are, not surprisingly, more concerned with the emotional side of issues or decisions. An F is more apt to ask how you feel than what you think, to look at the effect of a choice on an individual's circumstances, and to say things like, "My gut tells me..." or "I don't feel right about this" or "I feel sad that..."

Imagine two characters on opposite ends of the T/F scale arguing about a social issue. Not only would their views differ, in some ways they wouldn't be speaking the same language.

Perceiving/Judging, on the other hand, is not quite as it sounds. A P tends to like things open ended. This person is more comfortable gathering information and keeping options open than making a final choice. A Judge feels better once a decision is made and likes clear answers.

Imagine characters at opposite ends of the P/J spectrum running a business or raising children together. They might complement each other, each one filling in for the other's challenges. On the other hand, they might drive each other crazy.

You can learn more about this personality theory and take the test yourself (or for your characters) at the Myers & Briggs Foundation website.

Before you do, though, off the top of your head (or based on your gut feeling, if you're an F), which is your character more apt to be:

Extroverted (E) or Introverted (I)?
Intuition (N) or Sensing (S)?
Thinking (T)/Feeling (F)?
Perceiving (P)/Judging (J)?
Does your character fall at the extreme for any of the above?
Which ones?
Can you create other characters who might fall at opposite ends of these personality types?

Some other personality theories and inventories you may want to check out include:

- The Big Five Personality Domains, which covers Extroversion; Agreeableness; Conscientiousness;

Neuroticism/Emotional Stability; Openness to Experience
- The Hexaco Personality Inventory, which focuses on Honesty-Humility; Emotionality; Extroversion; Agreeableness/Anger; Conscientiousness; and Openness to Experience.
- Enneagrams, which divide people into 9 personality types such as Adaptive Peacemaker and Quiet Specialist.

QUICK GUIDE: PERSONALITY TYPES

- Personality types, tests, and theories can help you explore your character's mind, heart, and way of interacting with others
- Creating characters who fall at opposite ends of particular traits is a great way to build conflict
- Personality theories/tests you may want to check out include the work of Myers and Briggs, the Big Five Personality Domains, the Hexaco Personality Inventory, and Enneagrams

11

RACE, ETHNICITY, AGE, GEOGRAPHY, AND GENDER

I've grouped these factors because they are ways that society categorizes people and that we categorize ourselves. They matter because your character doesn't exist in a social vacuum. Even a character alone on a deserted island probably interacted with people at some point in the past or will in the future.

I've placed this section fairly late in the book, however, because individuals of the same race, ethnicity, gender, background, age, etc., vary widely from one another. What will make your characters real is understanding what makes them tick and how they act, and that might or might not correlate to the categories a person checks off on a census form.

Geography

That is what I didn't take long enough to consider. I simply assumed I would bundle up my New York wife with her New York interests, her New York pride, and remove her from her New York parents—leave the frantic, thrilling future land of Manhattan behind—and transplant her to the little town on the river in Missouri, and all would be fine.

Gone Girl, Part One, Nick Dunne, The Day Of

The above passage shows the significance of geography in ***Gone Girl***.

Nick's and Amy's marriage wasn't going great while they were in Manhattan. They'd lost their jobs. Also, Amy had dropped her "Cool Girl" act, which was what drew Nick in. She started behaving, to her mind, as herself, and she felt Nick no longer loved her and that he stopped making an effort in the relationship.

But the death blow was moving from Manhattan to small town Missouri.

Amy puts on a show of fitting in, mainly so she can mess with Nick later from beyond the grave, so to speak. But she feels completely out of place there. In her fake diary, she writes about the first party where everyone brings food in plastic containers. She recycles them and is surprised to find everyone expects them washed and returned. She reads judgment on their faces when she admits she didn't understand that.

She also has nothing to do in Missouri. She wrote quizzes for magazines in New York, but most magazine writing jobs have disappeared. Nick's job has disappeared as well, but because Amy is so out of her element she's adrift in Missouri. Nick at least becomes an adjunct professor at a local college and opens a bar with his sister. Amy's quiz writing doesn't lend itself to anything in the small town, and certainly not anything that brings her into contact with anyone else.

Even the furniture moved from New York doesn't fit. There's a wonderful description of the sofa sitting:

> ...in the living room looking stunned, as if it got sleep-darted in its natural environment and woke up in this strange new captivity, surrounded by faux-posh carpet and synthetic wood and unveined walls.

Gone Girl, Amy Elliott Dunne, October 16, 2010, Diary Entry.

The questions to ask yourself about geography are no different from the ones already covered in this book. Take a look back—particularly at Chapters 7-9—and ask yourself whether or how your answers would change if your character lived in a different location from the one you first envisioned.

If you didn't have a particular locale in mind, take time to imagine one and review the questions again.

∼

Race

Writing characters of a race other than your own can feel filled with minefields, in part because even a sentence like this one raises questions, starting with **What is race? How is it defined?**

Or, more to the point, are there actually different "races"? I never heard anyone ask this question when I was a kid, but scientists today say race is a cultural construct "without biological meaning."

Even as a cultural construct, the generally-accepted answers to questions about race change over time. When I was a kid, census forms had different—and more limited—racial categories. People also held different beliefs about what traits or genetic factors meant someone belonged to one race or another.

Also, in life and fiction, how a person identifies himself varies. Two characters with similar backgrounds might see themselves as having different identities.

As an example from life, The Miller Center describes the parents of the 44th president of the United States, Barack Obama, as follows: "His parents, who met as students at the University of Hawaii, were Ann Dunham, a white American from Kansas, and Barack Obama, Sr., a black Kenyan studying in the United States."

In fiction, one character with these same parents might identify as black, another as white, and others in any number of different ways.

These include questions that touch on geographic identification. African-American? American? Kansan? African? Kenyan?

Does your character identify as a certain race?

If so, how does the character identify and why?

If not, why?

How do other people who know the character well identify her?

How do people who meet your character once identify him?

How does your character feel about all of the above?

You as the author need to think about questions of race for your character to be believable, even if your character never thinks about it, because that in itself is significant. It is typically only people who fit into the majority in a culture who are able to opt not to think about their racial identities.

The issue of your characters' racial identities also raises challenges because there are many different opinions about authors writing about people different from themselves. Particularly when the only way to get a book into the hands of readers was through a publishing company, many writers and readers raised concerns about people who were part of the dominant culture controlling the portrayal of people who were not. There also are concerns about profiting off experiences not your own or making mistakes in portraying people of other races, ethnicities, or cultures.

At the same time, including only people of

your own race and background (however you define both) can be unrealistic and can make for a dull book. It also can limit the diversity of characters portrayed throughout literature as a whole.

While I've not found a clear answer to the ethical questions, you can minimize some of the troubling issues by striving to create well-developed, three-dimensional characters, whether you use the techniques in this book or find another way.

Also, any time you're writing about a community or an experience with which you are unfamiliar, you need to do research. You can't assume that someone who identifies racially as you do would have the same experience as you, nor that all people of a different racial identity would have the same experience as one another. So read, talk with people, watch videos, and do your best to learn as much as you can as you create your characters and story. This will give you a wider knowledge base from which to draw to create each unique character.

Further, if you're writing about an experience more familiar to you, take whatever extra steps you need to authentically portray a character from a different background. A character of another race may be more likely than you to experience certain obstacles or advantages, and you want to do enough research to be aware of that. The research may or may not filter into your writing, and your character may or may not have a "typical" experience, to the extent there is such a thing, but you'll be making an informed choice.

Take a moment to look back at the questions in previous sections and ask yourself whether or how the character's racial identity affects the answers.

~

Ethnicity

Your character's ethnic background may or may not be significant for that person and for those around him. In the suburb where I grew up, many people were only a generation or two from immigrating to the United States. Many, like my mom's family, came from Poland, but many also were from Ireland, Italy, and what was once Bohemia.

My dad's family was primarily English in origin, but as a kid it didn't occur to me that it influenced at all who my dad was as a person, as our extended family on his side lived across the country. But as an adult when I began learning more about English culture, I discovered there were traits that, at least to my writer's mind, might be traced back to that, such as stoicism, reserve, and a tendency toward understatement.

The first time I dated someone from an Italian family, I was a bit overwhelmed. His parents waved their arms, yelled, and proclaimed their opinions and their love loudly and often.

Obviously, not all people of Italian origin are expressive or demonstrative and not all people descended from the English are reserved. And not everyone who shares any of those traits attributes it to ethnicity rather than to individual personality traits and preferences. **What matters is not your character's ethnicity but whether and how that character perceives ethnicity as influencing people, including herself.**

If you're unsure, research the history of people of different ethnicities living in the region where your character lives. Whether or not the research makes its way into your story, it'll make your characters richer.

Below are a few questions to ask yourself. As with the other questions in this book you need not know all the answers, but this will give you a start.

Where were your character's parents born?

How many generations of your character's family (if any) have lived in the region where your character lives now?

What is the ethnic make up of the region where your character now lives?

How strongly, if at all, does your character identify with his current region or country?

Is there another region or country with which your character identifies?

How strongly, if at all, does your character identify with her ethnic heritage?

As you did with geography and race, review the questions and answers from earlier chapters with ethnicity in mind. (If you accounted for that when thinking about geography and race, no need to do it again.)

If you didn't but you don't want to go through all the questions again, you can instead look at each chapter heading and ask yourself how ethnicity might play into that topic as a whole.

∽

Age

As my parents neared retirement age, my mom always said, "Old is ten years older than you are." You can as easily substitute "middle age" for "old" depending on where you are in life. Either sentence is a good way to sum up how people's beliefs about age factor into how they feel and how others see them.

Comedian George Burns, who lived to be 100, commented that some people start "practicing" to be old early on. They hit sixty and start taking small steps and groaning when they rise from a chair. Whether or not their body has changed significantly, they believe it has and must. They feel old.

Others take my mom's view and simply never feel old absent serious health issues. Or sometimes even with serious health issues.

That's not to say there aren't any differences based on age regardless of the character's attitude. Your character's frame of reference will change. Does he remember living through World War II, the fall of the Soviet Union, 9/11?

Going back to physical health, statistically speaking older characters are more likely to have serious health issues, as well as various aches and pains, than are younger ones. But this varies widely from person to person and so from character to character.

You can write about an eight-year-old child fighting cancer or an eighty-year-old woman running a marathon, and both those life events likely

Creating Compelling Characters

will be more of a factor in how that character sees life than will age alone.

All the same, while health and physical well-being need not be a function of age, age will likely affect how that character sees himself in comparison with others.

An eighty-year-old character diagnosed with cancer will be more likely to know others in the same age range with the same diagnoses, including those who survived and those who died. An eight year old will not. This may cause the eight-year-old character (or that character's parents) to feel more singled out and isolated than the eighty year old.

Characters also will be treated differently by others depending upon their age or the age they appear to be. In the workplace, people who are young or young-looking often struggle to be taken seriously, while people who are nearing retirement age (or look it) may find others treating them as if they're already on the way out the door regardless of their actual intentions.

Technology changes also affect characters. If you are writing a twenty-something character living in the U.S. earning an average income who never uses a cell phone, you'll need to explain why. Shift the same character to ninety, and you probably don't need to make a particular point about that.

It's also worth reading a few articles about generational differences in attitude, hopes, ambitions, and stressors. Those of us who grew up playing outside every summer day and freely roaming the neighborhood until dark might need insight into the generation of children with scores of planned activities that dictated their parents' schedules. Those who reached their forties or fifties before 9/11 in the U.S. might not grasp how the non-stop television coverage of planes flying into the Twin Towers affected someone who was ten at the time.

As with any other factor, though, each character is more than her age. It's a trait to keep in mind, and it matters, but there's no need to be hamstrung by preconceptions about how someone of a particular age feels, looks, or acts.

That being said, a few points to think about:

How does your character feel about being her particular age?

Some kids enjoy being kids, others can't wait to grow up. Some people begin lamenting getting older as soon as they hit twenty-one, others feel young at seventy. Some people are conscious of each change in their health and attribute it to age,

Creating Compelling Characters

assuming everything's downhill from here, others don't feel age makes that much difference.

How old are most of your characters' friends?

Does the character have friends from different generations?

Either way, how does that affect the character?

What's the age difference between your character and his parents?

How does that affect the character?

Is your character dealing with any age-related health conditions?

What does the character believe about "old people"?

About the next generation?

About "kids today"?

How long does your character believe she will likely live?

Does your character embrace new technology?

Why or why not?

Does your character believe life has gotten better or worse over time?

Gender

Many authors successfully write about protagonists and antagonists with a different gender from their own. And all authors, unless they're writing about a community of Amazons or the like, need to write at least some characters of different genders.

Here, too, what matters is creating a compelling and believable character, not whether your character is "like a real woman" or "like a real man."

Nonetheless, it can help to read articles, blog posts, and/or non-fiction books on issues that touch on your story and also deal with gender or that specifically address gender questions.

For instance, if you're writing about lawyers or businesspeople, you might want to read *What Works For Woman At Work* or other similar books. It will give you insight into challenges women in general face in those environments, as well as into the pluses many men may experience, often without being aware of them.

But you don't need to lift your character from the pages of someone else's book or blog, nor does your character need to represent a "typical" man or woman if there is such a thing. Gillian Flynn said she gave Nick Dunne her own background and her own experience of coming to New York

Creating Compelling Characters

from the Midwest and also of losing her job as the publishing industry changed. It didn't matter that Nick was a male character and Gillian Flynn a female author. The feelings of not fitting in and about loss of job and identity rang true.

Deliberately writing against gender expectations also can be compelling. When Sara Paretsky started her V.I. Warshawski series, almost all private investigators in fiction were men. She specifically set out to write a female private detective and to address the gender issues women faced.

If you do this, or if you're writing a character whose choices would be likely to get pushback for reasons of gender, be sure to consider how that will affect your character's relationships, family, work, and other aspects of the character's personal and professional life.

Also, keep in mind that readers don't live in a social vacuum. Whether it's fair or not, if you have a character who acts, thinks, or feels differently from readers' expectations about gender, you may need to include a few more details than you otherwise would to support it.

Finally, while I personally find it hard to read books that rely heavily on gender stereotypes, and it's a good rule to avoid them, plenty of stories are wildly successful with characters that to me read more like caricatures. I hope you won't choose to write that way. But I mention it so that you won't feel the world will end—or you should abandon your efforts—if you don't succeed in making every character three-dimensional and in avoiding all stereotypes.

Take a look at the questions in previous chapters.

Would any of your answers change if you switched the gender of your character?

Which ones and how?

QUICK GUIDE: RACE, ETHNICITY, AGE, GEOGRAPHY, AND GENDER

- There can be as much variation among people of the same race, gender, ethnicity, etc., as there is among people who fall under different categories
- There is no "typical" character of a certain age, ethnicity, gender, etc.
- Research to be sure you're aware of particular challenges or advantages characters may have based on demographic factors
- Ask yourself whether the answers to the questions in this book would change if you changed your

L. M. LILLY

character's geographic location, gender, race, or ethnicity

12

MUST YOUR CHARACTER BE LIKABLE?

Writers often struggle with whether the protagonist and other major characters (other than the antagonist) need to be "likable." A close second is whether the protagonist needs to be "relatable."

Those words are in quotes because they mean something different to every writer, reader, and literary critic who uses them, which makes it hard to give a definitive answer.

Still, I'll take a shot at it:

Likable: No, but

Relatable: Yes, but

Okay, not that definitive. I'll do my best to clarify in the sections below.

Likable vs. Intriguing

The "but" in likable means it depends on the genre. You're more apt to find likable protagonists in romance, horror, thrillers, and mystery because you as a reader need to root for the protagonist. It's easier to root for a character you like.

Also, a fast-paced, plot-oriented novel or story allows less time and space for the reader to get to know a character who might be unlikable but nonetheless interesting.

Despite all of the above, though, and no matter the type of story, an unlikable character can serve as a protagonist if the reader nonetheless wants to spend a lot of time with that character. Put another way, readers will pay to read about characters they like again and again, but they'll also pay to read about characters they don't like but who intrigue them.

The Dead Zone features a very likable protagonist. John Smith has a good sense of humor and is easygoing and fun. He cares about his students, he learns all their names early in the semester, and they behave well for him. He's down-to-earth, and as the book continues we see that he strives to do the right thing even at great personal cost. He's not

Creating Compelling Characters

perfect, and he struggles with his temper from time to time, but he's a guy in real life you'd enjoy knowing.

As in real life, though, a character need not be likable to be intriguing. Think about a real person who fascinates you but whom you don't necessarily like, or at least who isn't generally considered likable.

You might want to spend time with that person for any number of reasons. Maybe you're both deeply committed to the same cause. Maybe he knows volumes about a topic that interests you and the two of you find yourself talking for hours. Maybe he is simply the one person who gets why this issue matters so much to you.

Maybe there's something about that person's upbringing that matches yours and you feel at ease with that person. Maybe the person is witty and insightful and you enjoy great conversations.

Maybe you feel driven to figure out what makes that person tick.

Nick Dunne provides an example of this last option in ***Gone Girl***. When we first meet him, he's tense and anxious on his anniversary, and we wonder why. He's also struggling to understand his wife, but he doesn't quite tell us the real reason. When she's missing and there's blood on the floor, the reader can't help but wonder if Nick was involved. He seems disturbed, he seems to be in shock, yet he also might only be worried about getting caught. He lies to the police, but it might be out of insecurity rather than guilt. We wonder which.

Is Nick a killer, a grieving husband, a philanderer, a guy who is clueless about who his wife really is? All of the above?

We don't like Nick, but we want to spend time with him to figure him out.

Amy as we first meet her—the Amy reflected in her fake diary—is very likable. Amy the character specifically crafts her own imaginary personality so her readers, who she expects to be the police and the public, will like her.

Both times I read the book, I felt less engaged once the "real" Amy started telling her story. Part of it is that I don't like that Amy, and I don't care that much what happens to her, though I did occasionally have empathy for her.

That being said, she's still pretty fascinating.

Sara Paretsky's V.I. Warshawki, who broke ground as the first fictional female private eye, lives in the middle ground on likability. She's a character many readers love and like, but whom others find too abrasive and hot headed to want to read about.

It's true that V.I. has a quick temper, tends to leap first and ask questions later, and often hurls accusations when a more open mind and less abrasive approach might work better.

But these qualities all arise from how deeply V.I. cares about the people who come to her for help and people whom others step on or ignore. She is passionately committed to achieving justice and finding answers. She's also fiercely loyal to her friends. She stands by what she believes and will put her own life at risk to help someone who needs it. These are all reasons I really like V.I., as do many readers, and it's why we buy book after book about her.

As V.I.'s example shows, what's likable is subjective. By and large, though, likability turns on how the character treats others. We like Johnny because we see him trying to ensure Sarah has a good time, trying to help people through his psychic power even when they initially reject him, and caring deeply about his mom and dad.

Likability often also comes with a character's willingness to be vulnerable. Johnny is honest and open with Sarah about how he feels about her despite that she's a little unsure about him and he knows that.

Elizabeth Bennet is vulnerable in a different way. She's willing to risk poverty rather than marry solely for fortune. She's also willing to say what she thinks and do what she believes is important (such as walking for miles alone in the country to see her ill sister) even where it invites the disdain of others.

Being likable can make it much easier to engage readers, but it's not necessary. Your character will, however, almost always need to be relatable.

∼

To Whom Do You Relate?

Relatability gets a bad rap, which is why the **Yes, but** answer.

A "relatable" character is often thought of as one whom the reader can easily imagine being. Under the most narrow definition, a thirty-something middle class white woman would only read books about other thirty-something middle class white women. Or if she wanted to push her boundaries, maybe she'd read about twenty-something or forty-something white women or about white men.

Creating Compelling Characters

This is part of why in the U.S. so many children's books for so long featured only white characters. The assumption was that children would only relate to characters who looked like them in terms of skin color, or at least that the parents who bought those books would believe that. The U.S. was predominantly white, so to sell to the greatest number the books featured white characters.

There also was a time when publishers were certain that while girls could relate to boy main characters, it did not work the other way around. So the main characters were more apt to be boys, again to sell to the greatest number.

What these assumptions have in common is the view that to find a character relatable, a reader must see herself in the character in certain demographic ways, such as economic status, race, ethnicity, cultural heritage, gender, and age.

While the world is moving away from these types of assumptions, there remains a view of "relatable" as meaning that you at least relate to the situation the character is in. So you could be a different gender or race from Othello or from Desdemona, Othello's wife and unfortunate victim. But both are relatable in that their story involves insecurity, jealousy, and domestic violence—issues with which modern readers remain familiar.

In both these senses of the word, your characters don't need to be relatable. Now more than ever readers and viewers are willing to immerse themselves in the experiences of people they perceive as not like themselves in many ways.

Also, those concepts of relatability had more to do with marketing than with whether a story or protagonist worked. Because people can now buy from authors without an intervening publisher, authors aren't limited to types of books or characters that publishers feel are sure bets or will appeal to huge numbers of people.

Finally, though, true relatability doesn't mean the character needs to be just like the reader or be facing a specific situation the reader can imagine being in. **It means the reader empathizes with the feelings the character has and the struggles the character faces, whether or not the reader ever expects to share the exact circumstances.**

In *Gone Girl*, for example, we see Nick struggling with how he fears people see him and how he feels inside. He knows he often appears arrogant, so he smiles to try to seem like a nice guy. He takes the extra step to be polite. But this turns out terribly when, realizing he's sounding wooden and unemotional, he smiles at a press conference when talking about his wife being missing. It bites him again when a pretty woman flirts with him at a refreshment table during a search party's efforts to find Amy. The woman cloaks her flirting in the guise of offering sympathy and insists on taking a selfie of the two of them. Nick complies despite alarm bells in his head because he wants to be polite, to seem like a nice guy.

When he sees the woman again, he rebuffs her, partly out of fear of looking bad. She's angry, so she shares the photo and professes shock that he flirted with her.

Again, at this point, I still don't know if he's a killer. I also don't expect ever to be in that situation. Yet I feel for Nick. He knows he's not coming off well, he tries to make it better, and no matter what he does, it's the wrong thing. That's a feeling I can empathize with and that probably all readers can understand. And it's amped up by the fact that Nick's very life may depend on what certain people, such as the police, the media, and a future jury, will think of him.

In addition, Nick desperately does *not* want to be like his father, who hates women and is nasty and abusive, and his greatest fear is that he is. While not everyone has had Nick's exact experience, many people fear sharing or inheriting their parents' worst traits.

Despite how extreme her behavior is, it's also possible to relate to Amy. Her parents made a lot of money writing children's books about Amazing Amy, who does everything ten times better than the real Amy and succeeds wherever Amy fails. No matter what else you feel or think about Amy at that moment, it's hard not to wonder what that does to a child. And who hasn't failed to live up to parents' expectations or disappointed them somehow?

~

Your Characters

To help ensure your characters are intriguing, relatable, or likable consider the following:

What is your character passionate about?

Johnny Smith loves teaching and has a gift for it. It makes him happy, and we see the young man he tutors excelling thanks to Johnny.

V.I. feels strongly about helping David slay Goliath. She sees authorities and people or companies with great wealth and resources oppressing others, and she jumps in on the side of those who are struggling.

Amy is obsessed with playing mind games and

manipulating others, and she is a master at it. It's not admirable, but it's fascinating all the same.

Nick desperately wants to be a better man than his father.

Whom does your character care most about and why?

Nick loves his twin sister, Go. Johnny loves Sarah and his parents. Amy, in her own twisted way, cares deeply about Nick. V.I. loves her friends and her neighbor, Mr. Contreras, who is like a grandfather to her, and her dogs.

What drives your character?

This question is similar to goals, but it includes the character's overall motive, which might or might not be conscious. Nick is driven to show the world he's not like his father, and to become a better man than his father. V.I. seeks justice and truth. Johnny strives for a normal life and, later, is driven to protect the world by stopping Stillson. Amy's obsessed with being loved for who she is.

In addition to the questions in this chapter, all the questions and prompts in this book can help make your character intriguing. If you feel your characters aren't likable, relatable, or intriguing enough, revisit them and fill in what's missing or experiment with changes.

QUICK GUIDE: LIKABILITY AND RELATABILITY

- A character, including a protagonist, need not be likable, though likability may make it easier to draw the reader in, especially in certain genres
- Your main character does need to be intriguing
- Readers want to relate to your main characters, but relatability need not be based on similar demographic factors (like age or gender)
- A character is relatable if the reader empathizes with the character's feelings and struggles, regardless whether the reader expects ever to be in a similar situation

13

WHAT'S IN A NAME

Most of this book is about what's happening in your characters' minds and hearts. But exploring characterization also requires talking about names.

Names offer cues to your reader as to each character's personality and background. They hint at the type of story you're telling. Compare a description of a high fantasy novel versus a mystery set in present day in the U.S.

You can pretty easily guess which is which by the character names.

A character's name also affects how you as the author feel about, and how you see, that character.

That's why although you could write Character

A, Character B, etc., as you plot and write your story, most writers have no desire to do that.

None of the above means you should spend hours, days, or weeks searching for the absolute correct name for your characters before starting to write. It's too easy for that to become an excuse to delay or avoid writing.

Instead, you can choose first draft, or placeholder, names.

That frees you to experiment and see how well the names work as your story and characters evolve. A character name that strikes you as perfect now may not work for you by the time you reach your story's halfway point.

If you like the names, though, you can keep them, with a few caveats that are covered in the chapter on final names below. If you don't, you can change them any time until the moment your book or story is published.

So let's talk about where to get ideas for first draft names. (If you're happy with a set of first draft names you already have, feel free to skip to the chapter on final names, though you might want to at least skim the following sections.)

∽

People You Know

In a first draft, you can borrow names from people you know. Rather than using full names, which has a few drawbacks we'll talk about below, borrow a first, middle, or last name.

The trick is to choose someone who evokes a feeling or image in your mind, but whom you don't know so well that the real person limits the character you create.

For instance, if for one semester in high school you sat next to the class clown, you might use that person's name for a particularly funny character. Assuming you didn't know the person well, you're free to invent whatever else you need for your character in addition to the sense of humor.

In contrast, let's say you borrow the name of Bettina, your best friend throughout grade school and high school, who was the funniest person you've ever known. If the Bettina in your story needs to have a hidden mean streak, it might be hard for you to include that if the real Bettina was a kind person. So it's better to name your funny character after someone you didn't know so well.

Even in a first draft, using the full name of anyone you know is usually a bad idea. If it slips through in your final draft that could be upsetting to the person, which will be on your mind as you

Creating Compelling Characters

write, and it will distract you. Also, as with the Bettina example, you'll be too inclined to write who you think that person really is rather than to create your own unique character.

Mixing up first, middle, and last names of real people, though, can be a good way to draw from real life but still create a unique character name.

If your childhood friend's full name was Bettina Wells, your lab partner was Jean Sorento, and you really like the actress Sarah Michelle Gellar (as I do), right there you have many name options.

If you want a name with alliteration, there's Sarah Sorento. For a three-name combo, try Bettina Michelle Wells or Jean Gellar Sorento. If you want a name with few syllables because for you that evokes someone who is plain spoken or strong, try Jean Wells.

List three first names of people you know and the positive traits you associate with them.

List three first names of people you know and the negative traits you associate with them.

Would you use any of these names in your first draft?

Why or why not?

Answer the same questions about last names.

Public Figures

You also can borrow names from actors and other public figures for your first draft. Because you don't know them personally, you'll feel fairly free to invent personality traits and histories for the characters.

Also, for actors or other entertainers, you've probably seen the person play different parts. That gives you more freedom, and a lot of ideas, when creating the character.

Think about your main characters. Are there any actors that, in your mind, the characters look like?

Are there personality traits of characters (or actors) from television or movies that make you think of your character?

When I was growing up, the stereotypical strong, silent tough guy was Clint Eastwood. If I were writing that type of character, I might name him Clint in a first draft, drawing from any number of books or movies that featured the actor.

When you get to your final draft, though, it's best not to use exact full names without permission. There may be legal issues, and it may confuse your readers.

An exception is if you're having your fictional

characters cross paths with an actual celebrity or public or historical figure.

In *The Dead Zone*, Johnny Smith shakes the hand of then-candidate Jimmy Carter and tells him he'll become president, though the vote will be close. This incident bolsters the reader's belief in Johnny's psychic ability, as the reader knows that Carter did become president.

Even with a cameo appearance, be cautious in your final draft, especially if you write anything unflattering. In the United States it's fairly difficult for a public figure to win a lawsuit over what someone writes, but it's not impossible. Other countries have stronger laws protecting public figures (and private individuals).

∼

Name Lists

Lists of names are a good place to get ideas, and you can find them all over the Internet. Try searching for popular baby names, uncommon baby names, baby names by gender, or baby names starting with a particular letter. You can also search for names by ethnicity, geography, or race.

Name lists by year are good resources. (To

check this out, try searching for the most popular baby names from the year you were born. This is also a fun way to see how creative, or not, your parents were when they named you.)

Choosing a fairly common name for a particular year can help give your readers an immediate sense of a character's age. In the United States, a character named Tiffany is likely to be younger than one named Gertrude. Chloe is probably younger still.

You can also try the types of sources that I used when I started writing and the Internet wasn't that accessible to ordinary people. (Yes, yes, it was a long time ago.) Looking at print phone books at a library allows you to scan tons of names of people from different backgrounds and pick ones that look interesting. Today's newspaper also will include many names of well-known and lesser-known people and reporters.

The biography and memoir sections in bookstores (brick-and-mortar or on-line) offer more ideas, as do the (first) names of students in your or your kids' (or friends' kids') classes, rosters for community organizations, or names of employees if you work at a large company.

Borrowing From Other Stories

There's nothing wrong with borrowing names from other stories you love, as long as you don't take the exact name. (Doing that might confuse the reader or violate the author's rights.)

Stories you can draw from include, among other things, novels, movies, television series, fables, and myths.

When I was searching for a name for the main character in my *Awakening* supernatural thriller series, I wanted something that fit the story. The protagonist is a young woman who becomes pregnant through supernatural means in Book 1. While not a religious story, the novel explores the role of religion, particularly male-dominated religion, in the world.

For that reason, I checked out the names of different goddesses. I chose Tara partly because that is the name of a mother goddess.

Similarly, I'm convinced, though I have no evidence, that the creator of my favorite television series *Buffy The Vampire Slayer* was a fan of *The Bionic Woman*.

Creator Joss Whedon is about my age, and *The Bionic Woman* was a popular show when we were kids. It featured a superpowered young woman with a bubbly personality who was kind and had a strong network of friends, family, and work colleagues.

That sounds a lot like Buffy Summers.

The *Bionic Woman*'s name? Jaime Sommers.

~

Symbolism

Sometimes you'll deliberately choose a name that symbolizes or conveys to others a certain trait, ideology, or type of person. I notice authors doing this most often when I'm reading literary fiction or fantasy, but it can be a factor in any type of story.

The protagonist of *The Dead Zone* is John Smith. Choosing a name frequently used to refer to Everyman conveys a great deal about him. Until the accident that puts him into a coma, Johnny's pretty much a regular guy. He's a teacher and recent college graduate in a small town. His dad is a carpenter and his mom stayed at home. He's easygoing, and he takes the woman he's dating to the county fair for a date. His psychic power when the book starts amounts to no more than the hunches or intuitions that any of us has from time to time.

King no doubt chose this name to convey that Johnny could be any one of us and to help put us into Johnny's mind as he faces terrible choices.

Another great example from popular culture is the television series *Lost*. Many of its characters are named for philosophers (Hume, Bentham, Locke, Rousseau, and others), which adds layers to the storylines and themes.

∾

Random

You can also simply choose a name from the figurative hat. You can take it off an advertisement on a bus or borrow a name you hear shouted as you pass a school yard.

A favorite side character for many readers of John Sandford's long-running ***Prey*** series is Dell.

What's Dell's last name?

Capslock.

You have to think Sandford came up with that while staring at the keyboard of a Dell computer. Nonetheless, Dell is a memorable character. If Sandford did pick the name from his computer keyboard, it didn't do any harm.

What matters is that your character has a name, any name, so you can write about that person. So long as there's nothing about the name that bothers you or distracts you, go ahead and use it.

The Nuts And Bolts Of Using First Draft Names

As you write, keep a list of names you think you'll want to change or any concerns you have about certain names. Doing this keeps you from being preoccupied with remembering to make changes later. It also helps you continue writing the first draft rather than stopping to change a name that starts to feel wrong.

Once in a while as you write you'll realize a name feels so wrong it keeps you from getting into your character. Switch to a different name midstream and see how that goes, adding a note or comment in your draft or on your list so you'll remember to fix it later.

I don't recommend going back to the beginning and changing the name right away. It's too easy to start rewriting the entire book, which slows down the first draft. (Your process may be different than mine, though, so if you need to use Find and Replace to put in the new name, go ahead and do it. Just try not to get bogged down in revisions.)

Once you've finished your first draft, you can figure out which names to keep and which to change.

QUICK GUIDE: FIRST DRAFT NAMES

- Don't strive for perfection
- Think of them as placeholder names to be improved later if needed
- Check lists of baby names
- Check lists of names from various countries
- Draw from people you know (though not their full, exact names)
- Draw from public figures (again, not exact names)
- Borrow from movies, books, and series you love (same caveat)
- Pick a name at random (from advertising, for example)

- **Remember you can always change it later!**

14

WHAT TO WATCH FOR WITH FINAL NAMES

Once you finish your story, set it aside. Wait at least a week to look at it again. (A month is even better for seeing it with fresh eyes, but your production schedule might not allow that.)

When you do read it, circle, highlight, or note any names you didn't like or that don't feel right. Also check with your list of names to see which ones troubled you as you were first drafting.

If your first draft/placeholder names work for you, you may want to keep them. Before you do, though, you'll want to look for a few issues.

Start by ensuring your list of character names is complete. This is especially important if you're writing a series. It will be hard later to remember all your character names off the top of your head. Ideally, use a format that allows sorting in alphabetical order by both first and last name.

Now check for the issues below. Read your list aloud if that helps.

~

FIRST LETTERS

Using too many names that start with the same letter makes it harder for readers to remember who is whom. The more characters your story includes, the more important this is, but it matters even if you have only a few.

Two main characters named Mike and Mordant or, worse, Mike and Mark can cause a lot of confusion. Don't make your reader work hard to enjoy your story.

If you're writing a series, you also need to watch this with minor characters. They may play small roles now, but could become important later.

In *The Awakening, Book 1,* without thinking much about it I named one of my protagonist Tara's sisters Kelly. I didn't expect Kelly to be more than a walk on part, and she was only mentioned once or twice.

Creating Compelling Characters

The second book began with a scene between Tara and another fairly major character, Kali. When I realized Tara's sister Kelly also would be an important part of Book 2, I could have kicked myself. That I had two "K" names hadn't hit me when writing Book 1 because Kelly played such a small part, but now I was stuck with them.

I worked very hard to differentiate Kelly and Kali, including cues to the reader about who was whom, in Books 2, 3, and 4. I've never gotten complaints about confusion, so it must have worked, but it took lot of extra time and energy.

∼

Names That Otherwise Sound Alike

You also want to avoid too many names that sound alike for reasons other than, or in addition to, the first letter.

First, Meg, Peg, Tig, and Tag may tend to blur in the readers' minds, as might the last names Martini, Gaddini, and Houdini. OK, maybe not the last since it calls to mind the famous magician, but you get the idea.

As I'm sure you noticed (but are too polite to say, right?), my Kelly/Kali problem suffers from the soundalike issue as well as the same first letter problem.

Second, it's boring. If all the names are Jane or John or Bob or Phil or Sue, it makes for a very dull book.

Third, it may be unrealistic, depending upon where your story takes place. If your characters live in a small town where many families are related and names tend to be used or reused over generations, a lot of similar names might be realistic. But if your story takes place somewhere like London that draws people from all over the world, it's likely there will be many names that sound different and are spelled differently from one another.

Race, Ethnicity, Geography

Names may signify to some readers ethnicity or race despite that in life names don't necessarily correlate with either. Many people have ancestors and family members of various ethnicities and/or marry into families from countries of origin other than their own. Also, as we talked about in Chapter Eleven, in reality the concept of race may signify nothing biological or genetic about a person.

All the same, if your character is named Brigid O'Brien, a picture of a white Irish woman will pop into many readers' mind. If you want to name your black Nigerian character that, feel free to do so, but you may need to add more description or narrative to convey how your character looks.

You may also need a "why" for those readers who have a set idea regarding names, race, and ethnicity. In other words, they'll want to know why your black Nigerian character has a very Irish-sounding name. Unless it's key to the plot, you'll need to find a quick way to do this without slowing your plot or boring those readers who don't care one way or the other.

All that being said, if one of your goals as a writer is to subvert and expand people's views on race, you may want to name your characters contrary to what most readers would expect. It's your story, so it's up to you to decide.

∼

Symbolic Names

Also take a look at those names you chose that were symbolic. Consider how many of these types of names you've used, and whether as a whole they'll be distracting.

This is particularly important if you're writing genre or commercial fiction. For those types of stories, your audience is not a class of college literature students searching for hidden meaning so they can add word count to their papers, and it's not the professors who teach them.

Your readers are ones who want to be absorbed in the story first and only later, perhaps, think about symbolism. **So if every character has a symbolic name, that will distract the reader rather than enhance the experience.** Even in *Lost*, where names of philosophers abound, many main characters have first names that are fairly common in Middle America like Kate, Jack, Ben, and Claire.

This doesn't mean you can't keep a symbolic name. But as a general rule, it's best to go for subtlety and be sparing rather than loading every character name with symbolic meaning.

∽

NUTS AND BOLTS Of Final Names

If you need to search for new names for your

Creating Compelling Characters

final draft, you can refer again to the sources in Chapter Thirteen.

Once you've chosen a new name for a character, try it out in a few scenes or a chapter. When you're happy with a name, use the Find and Replace function on your word processing program to replace the old with the new.

A few tips, though, for avoiding mishaps when you do:

- **Look out for names that are part of other words.**

For example, the name *Tom* is also in the word *atom* and *atomic*. If you use the global Find and Replace function to replace every *Tom* with *Erik*, *atom* and *atomic* will turn into *aeric* and *aericic*.

You can catch this problem by checking individually the first ten or twenty Find and Replace instances (rather than using a global "Replace All" strategy). When the *tom* part of *atom* gets highlighted, you'll discover the issue.

You can also limit this problem by using the Match Case option if it's available. (Usually it appears in a drop down menu.) That way you'll find *Tom* but not *tom*.

This won't catch everything, however. The sentence ***Tomatoes are in season.*** will become ***Ericatoes are in season.*** (This might lead to a story all its own, but is probably not what you're going for.)

To address this, you can search for ***Tom*** with a space after it. This avoids the ***Tomatoes*** problem. Remember, though, that this approach leaves off the name if punctuation appears after it, so you'll need to Find and Replace ***Tom, Tom. Tom's*** and so forth.

- **Search for the old names.**

Once you're done, do a Find to search for each old name to see if your replacement strategy missed anything. You'll be surprised how often that happens. You can fix the errors manually or formulate Find and Replace searches. Just keep an eye out for other errors you might accidentally introduce.

- **Replace names before other revisions.**

Both to help catch the ***Ericatoes*** problem and to see how well the names work, it's best to replace/fix all your names before you do other revisions in your draft. That way as you revise you'll spot errors caused by Find and Replace. You'll also get a better feel for how the new names work in the story as a whole.

- **Proofread (for real)**

Make sure you do a "real" proofread or have someone else do it for you. Spellcheck will only get you so far.

QUICK GUIDE: FINAL NAMES

- Watch for names with the same first letter
- Revise names that sound too much alike for any reason
- Consider your characters' ethnic backgrounds and racial identities
- Consider where your characters live
- Watch for unintended consequences of Find and Replace

15

LISTENING AND ICEBERGS

There's one thing you can do that will make more difference than everything else in this book. I'll go further—it's one thing that can take the place of everything in this book.

Listen.

When your friend or parent or partner wants to talk about her day, listen. Don't interrupt to share your thoughts, don't start immediately thinking about what you'll say when it's your turn, don't search your mind for a similar experience you've had that you're sure the other person will want to hear about.

Take a breath, focus on the other person, and listen.

Similarly, listen to your coworker, to that annoying person in the back of the train car talking too loud on the phone, and to someone talking on a YouTube video about a topic she is passionate about, especially if it's a topic that normally wouldn't interest you.

If someone says his day was "pretty good," ask what the best part of it was. Ask what the worst part was. Listen to the response. If you meet someone for the first time, and that person says she's a bookkeeper, ask what that's like. How did she choose that profession? What's fun about it? What's frustrating?

Don't ask simply to create an opportunity to shine yourself. Ask to listen and truly get to know this person.

If you make listening a habit, you'll learn more about character than you will if you answer a thousand questionnaires. (You'll also probably have more friends and better relationships, but that's a topic for a different book.)

Icebergs And Characterization

Before we close, you may be wondering how

much of what you've figured out about your characters should appear in the actual story.

Like so many things, the answer is "it depends."

If you're writing a fast-paced thriller, most of what you reveal about character will happen on the fly, sometimes literally. Perhaps 5% of what you know about your characters will make it into the story and the rest, like the bulk of an iceberg, will be invisible. Your readers won't expect scenes where a character thinks about, or talks to someone else about, her childhood, feelings, or decisions. In fact, one writing instructor I had advised me that in a thriller the author should cut out every scene where the character sits and thinks.

At the other end of the spectrum, some literary novels are essentially character studies with a bit of a story to organize them. Readers who love this type of book might be fine with spending half the book on a porch where two characters talk and the author details the stories of their lives starting at birth.

To make it more complicated, not only are there genres and books that fall everywhere in between on the spectrum, some stories run contrary to reader expectations.

Creating Compelling Characters

Typically, horror is fairly in-the-moment and fast moving. Yet Stephen King, considered the Master of Horror, has written books like **The Stand** and *It* where perhaps as much as half the novel could be dropped without harming the actual plot. (The books would not be as good, though, as many readers, including me, love King's work because of his characters.)

On the other hand, there are literary works where the author directly reveals next to nothing about the characters. In Ernest Hemingway's **Hills Like White Elephants** we never learn the male character's name, and we don't know the characters' ages or any of their backstory beyond what we can guess from the dialogue.

Your best approach is to include everything you feel is relevant or important in your first draft. As you rewrite, you can cut out the parts that strike you as unnecessary.

When you're ready, send the manuscript to a story editor and/or to beta readers (first readers who give you feedback). If any of them don't understand why a character does something or don't believe the character would take an action, and you're certain the character would, that's a sign that you need to include more about the character so the reader understands.

If they feel the book is too slow or note parts where they were tempted to put the book down (or did), you may have put in too much backstory.

Another good way to gauge how much to include is to choose a book that you like in your genre. Go through it and highlight those sections that reveal character. This should give you an idea both how and where character development is woven into the story and what percentage of the book is devoted mainly to character development. You can then use that as a guide for your own novel.

∼

More On Fiction Writing

My working title for this book was *Super Simple Character Creation* because it matched my previous book *Super Simple Story Structure: A Quick Guide to Plotting and Writing Your Novel.* As I wrote, though, I realized there's no step-by-step process, at least not one I know of, for creating characters the same way you plot a novel.

That's not a bad thing. In some ways, it makes creating characters a more relaxed, enjoyable process. It's creative and open-ended. You get to know your characters the way you do people in real life.

So I hope you'll have fun with your characters and with the questions and prompts in this book.

If you'd like help plotting or revising your novel, check out the free story story structure worksheets at **Help With Your Novel** on the website WritingAsASecondCareer.com.

You'll also find information there about getting individual feedback on your plot and about personal story coaching. And, for those who prefer online self-study courses, I created **How To Plot Your Novel: From Idea To First Draft**.

Whatever stage you're at with your fiction — planning, finished, or in between — thank you for letting me be part of your journey, and good luck with your next steps.

Did you enjoy this book and find it helpful? If so, please leave a review wherever you purchased it. Doing so will help other writers find the book. For more information on writing, marketing, and time management you can visit WritingAsASecondCareer.com.

ALSO BY L. M. LILLY

Super Simple Story Structure: A Quick Guide to Plotting and Writing Your Novel

The One-Year Novelist: A Week-By-Week Guide To Writing Your Novel In One Year

Creating Compelling Characters From The Inside Out

Write On: How To Overcome Writer's Block So You Can Write Your Novel

Happiness, Anxiety, and Writing: Using Your Creativity To Live A Calmer, Happier Life

Buffy And The Art Of Story Season One: Writing Better Fiction By Watching Buffy

Buffy And The Art Of Story Season Two Part 1

Buffy And The Art Of Story Season Two Part 2

How To Write A Novel, Grades 6-8

Writing as Lisa M. Lilly:

The Awakening (Book 1 in The Awakening Series)

The Unbelievers (Book 2 in The Awakening Series)

The Conflagration (Book 3 in The Awakening Series)

The Illumination (Book 4 in The Awakening Series)

The Complete Awakening Supernatural Thriller Series Box Set

When Darkness Falls (a standalone supernatural suspense novel)

The Tower Formerly Known As Sears And Two Other Tales Of Urban Horror

The Worried Man (Q.C. Davis Mystery 1)

The Charming Man (Q.C. Davis Mystery 2)

The Fractured Man (Q.C. Davis Mystery 3)

The Troubled Man (Q.C. Davis Mystery 4)

The Hidden Man (Q.C. Davis Mystery 5)

Q.C. Davis Mysteries 1-3 (The Worried Man, The Charming Man, and The Fractured Man) Box Set

ABOUT THE AUTHOR

An author, lawyer, and adjunct professor of law, L. M. Lilly's non-fiction includes *Super Simple Story Structure: A Quick Guide to Plotting and Writing Your Novel*; *The One-Year Novelist: A Week-By-Week Guide To Writing Your Novel In One Year*; *Happiness, Anxiety, and Writing: Using Your Creativity To Live A Calmer, Happier Life*; *Buffy And The Art Of Story Season One: Writing Better Fiction By Watching Buffy*; and *Creating Compelling Characters From The Inside Out*.

Writing as Lisa M. Lilly, she is the author of the bestselling *Awakening supernatural thriller series* about a young woman who becomes the foe of a powerful religious cult when she mysteriously finds herself pregnant, and of the *Q.C. Davis mystery series*, a traditional detective series set in Lilly's hometown of Chicago. She is currently working on the latest book in that series.

Lilly also is the author of *When Darkness Falls,*

a gothic horror novel set in Chicago's South Loop, and the short-story collection *The Tower Formerly Known as Sears and Two Other Tales of Urban Horror*, the title story of which was made into the short film Willis Tower.

She is the host of the podcast *Buffy and the Art of Story*. Find the podcast and her fiction at Lisa-Lilly.com.

www.WritingAsASecondCareer.com
Lisa@LisaLilly.com

www.ingramcontent.com/pod-product-compliance
Lightning Source LLC
Chambersburg PA
CBHW050317120526
44592CB00014B/1942